Welcome to Awakening

How to be Free in the Human Experience

by Renee Johanna

xoxo Renee Johanna

In Memory and Eternal Dedication

To Grandma Jo for saving my life and guiding me through my darkest days until I could see the light.

Especially to Kelli, my beautiful cousin and soul sister, for our real and raw conversations about life, love and the beyond. May your courageous battle forever enlighten and empower all who are brought to this message.

Acknowledgements

To my sons, Zach and Quade, for teaching me the true meaning of unconditional love.

To Randy for always being my best friend in love and life. Thank you for believing in me, long before I believed in myself.

To Mom for being my biggest fan, loudest cheerleader and strongest supporter of all my crazy dreams.

To Dad for showing me my own truth, strength and compassion.

To Esther Hicks and Abraham for life changing guidance from greater intelligence beyond the physical.

To the awake and aware, whom I call mind mates, for being the mirrors of my highest and best self. Thank you for inspiring the desire to let my free spirit fly.

Introduction

Who am I and why am I here?

Why does life seem so difficult for some
and not for others?

What is the key to happiness?

Will I find true and lasting love?

Do we really have free will or is someone/something
pulling the strings?

Where is our beginning and do we ever end?

What is the meaning of life???

Personally, I have been asking these questions, and questioning the answers, for my entire existence. Through the proof of my own experiences, as well as testimonials from the thousands of people I have consulted and connected with, each one of us has the same thing in common. No matter what has happened to us up to this point, or what we want to unfold in the future, we are the only ones who ultimately design our own destiny; and how happy we will be along the way.

We are the brilliant author of our own story, the incredible leading role in our own movie, and the gifted artist painting our masterpiece on a blank canvas; every new day. There is no future already mapped out for us, no hidden path to discover, and everything is created through the same universal laws and perfect timing for all of us. Unfortunately, many of us are still operating under the same outdated beliefs that I did for most of my days.

The biggest one was the illusion that life was happening to me, when it is actually responding to me.

Hello? I didn't get that memo until I had already spent an enormous amount of time, money, and energy looking in the wrong direction. I was hard at work surviving my own reality, while also attempting to make sense of it. Along the same lines, I believed the disempowering thought that told me it had to be another person, place, or something miraculous to line up first in order for me to truly be happy, joyous, and free.

Adding insult to injury, the biggest part of me has always had access to a bigger picture of wisdom. I just didn't know how to trust it when I was witnessing so many of my own family members drowning in their sorrows. I desperately wanted to believe the words of promise would match their actions, but they usually didn't. I wanted to believe the laughter and smiles instead of feeling their hidden pain, but I couldn't.

Unknowingly I was treating my own empathic intuition as an uncomfortable sensitivity I was plagued with. I wanted to experience the bliss of ignorance, but I could always sense more information than I really knew what to do with. After all, when so many grownups were in agreement about life being a bitch and then you die, who was I to think differently?

Growing up in an environment with loved ones who displayed the worst in human behavior, it was fairly easy to believe the entire world was a cruel and dangerous place. My Dad was extremely handsome and a gifted musician, among his other natural-born abilities. He lived the honkytonk life that country songs were made from. He was running around on my Mom and becoming violently abusive whenever she called him out on it; which was pretty much every weekend. When he was in sober remorse, he would hang his head in shame and give a stranger the shirt off his back to ease his guilt.

I have a long line of relatives who have experienced the same mental madness. Sadly, many still do. Those who never learn how to manage the brilliance of their own powerful light spend most of their time hiding in the dark. Our family legacy includes childhood trauma, torture, domestic violence, abuse, addiction, mental illness, ongoing health issues, and suicide. All in an effort to escape the torturous thoughts and negative emotional energy fueling our bodies. I could see myself in all of them and became horrified that I would eventually experience the same demise.

As a young girl, I always noticed the obvious truths that no one else was paying attention to. When I started to reveal my deepest insights, I only saw fear, confusion and even anger in the eyes looking back at me. I knew I was very different from anyone I was coming into contact with, and therefore I was determined to keep the secret hidden. I quickly learned to tell people what they wanted to hear rather than take the chance of being attacked or rejected for expressing what I could see and feel. I wanted to be anyone but me, and I gave up on the idea that I could ever change my mind about that decision.

Until I received divine intervention from Grandma Jo, short for Johanna; my very own maternal Grandmother. Through-out my entire childhood, we only lived a few miles apart and I spent as much time as possible with her. When I was with my Grandma, I was with my best friend and the safest shelter from any storm at home. We definitely had our share of heart to hearts when she was alive, but I had no idea just how special our bond will always be.

After several decades of seeking the ultimate authority on the planet who could help me understand what was wrong with me and my tortured loved ones, it was my Grandma Jo who would save the day once again. I was in my late 30s and about to face the worst nightmare I had experienced so far. My youngest son was barely a teenager and already showing signs and symptoms of following in the family footsteps of addic-tion. One night, as I was exhaustedly contemplating my own will to live again, Grandma Jo paid me a visit shortly after I had fallen asleep.

She woke me up, sat on my bed and began telling me about who I am and why I came here. Everything. Much like the beautiful puzzles we had spent countless hours putting together in my youth, she was now bringing to me the missing pieces that fit perfectly. Grandma told me I would need to trust myself completely, whether anyone believed me or not. She said I would need to learn how to live in the energy of pure love, especially if I wanted to stay connected with her.

Since I had spent most of my life chronically depressed and suicidal, this seemed utterly impossible for me to achieve. Grandma explained that the reason I would experience depression, or felt anxiously uncomfortable in my own skin, was because I was sensing and internalizing the thoughts and feelings of everyone around me. She said it was critical for me to learn how to separate my own mind and emotions from others. Grandma Jo insisted that I would need to stop resisting my intuition,which I know now is the strongest of all my senses and the part of me I unknowingly kept trying to shut down.

Everything was resonating on a deeper level. I started getting really excited that there might be more to my story than some sort of karmic punishment. The next morning, I opened my eyes and immediately started crying. I realized my Grandma had already died, and it was just a dream.

There were several more "visits" after that, and always when I needed her most. It was as if she had gone to the land of ultimate intelligence and was validating everything I always knew to be true, but struggled to believe. After years of searching for the right doctors and diagnoses, I was suddenly under the care of my dead Grandma Jo; and she was helping me more than anyone with a pulse. Of course, at the time, I told no one outside of my immediate family.

I started relaying significant dream messages from her to other loved ones who were in need. Ironically, the continuous validation from people who had always known me was actually helping me to stop questioning my own sanity, for the first time ever. A lifetime of crippling confusion was becoming clearer and clearer. I honestly didn't debate if it was really her, or my imagination creating her, I only cared that I was getting to stay in contact with Grandma Jo. She was not only saving my life, she was teaching me how to live it.

As a true bleeding heart who wanted to fix the world's problems, and love the broken back to wholeness, I finally realized the best example could be delivered through my own process of transformation. The time had come for me to start applying everything I had learned so far, from the inside out, and prove it could work, even for me. I knew this was the only way I was ever really going to be able to help my son, my other loved ones, or any other ESP (extra special person) like me.

Not only would I need to free myself from my own prison of pain, but I also had to learn how to allow my story to get better and better, completely releasing the dreaded false belief that eventually the "other shoe" would drop to squash my happiness again. Believe it or not, diving into rescue others from the seas of crisis and chaos became much easier than waiting for the next wave to knock me down.

True to my promises to Grandma Jo, I started learning how to follow my intuition instead of looking for solutions in the physical world. I deliberately focused my complete attention on filling myself up with better feeling thoughts, words and actions: about me. I began exploring mindfulness through yoga, meditation, and positive visualization; to unclutter my mind and calm my nervous energy.

The deeper I relaxed into pure nothingness, the more I connected to another dimension. Even when I wasn't sleeping, I was getting dream world communication from more loved ones who were transitioning. I was meeting all of them in a higher frequency of love and awareness; aka the other side. All of the so called "secrets" of the universe were suddenly so obvious. I had found the invisible door to a world that felt more like home than any place I had ever experienced on this planet.

Instead of making plans of action and to do lists, I started feeling my way to the next inspiring words and wisest teachers who offered a message I completely aligned with. I was drawn to more and more information about the power of positive belief, metaphysics, and the law of attraction. Each insightful master was confirming the same invisible information that I sensed so long ago. However, back then I didn't have the ability to understand that I was reading energy, nor the words to describe it; and neither did anyone else.

Within a few years, I was crossing paths with incredible minds who would not only validate my level of awareness, but could also mirror higher versions of me yet to be seen. I was finally having face-to-face contact with amazing human beings, who were living proof of the power of universal truth and positive belief in action. I knew I was no longer the exception to every rule, and I was more than ready to consciously participate in my own dreams.

It was also during this time of awakening, that I was inspired to write about it. A number of people soon began pointing out that I had a way with words, and the idea for this book was conceived. I felt like a newborn baby, in a 46-year-old body; eager to create an enlightened message for anyone it might help; possibly developing a template for the tortured, lost, and confused, to experience a different reality in this lifetime. The powerful alignment of an ultimate mind, with the intuitive wisdom of a thousand lifetimes.

I soon discovered I would not be able to move from one page to the next, unless I could integrate and live in the truth of every word I was writing. Since I had built my life on a faulty foundation of fear and negative thinking, topped with decades of running from an imaginary monster within, I obviously had a lot of clearing and cleansing to do. In order to be free, I had no choice but to live in unconditional love; from the inside out.

My intention, especially in writing this book, is to help light the way to the end of the tunnel, as well as how to adapt to a new reality, especially for those who are sick and tired of being sick and tired. What I didn't realize is that I would be the first recipient of everything I was translating. I literally wrote my way through my final transformation; to full awakening. Imagine my surprise, after spending most of my life searching for the cure to my curse, to find out that there was never anything wrong with me to begin with.

In 2014, with the encouragement and absolute belief of my loved ones, I was ready to start living my truth. Professionally,

I was still working hard at pretending to care about a stressful job in finance for an extremely conservative bank, mostly to keep the insurance going for my son's expensive trips to rehab or the hospital. For nearly two years I lived two different lives as I adjusted to truly being seen, after all of those years in hiding. I chose the perfect spot away from my so called "normal" life to release my fears and insecurities and into full belief of me.

I spent every weekend, holiday, and spare moment, "reading" and writing, in Jerome, Arizona; the best place on earth for spirits to be free. Founded in 1876, this tiny community of under 500 people, was once a booming copper mine but a series of natural (or supernatural) disasters left Jerome an abandoned ghost town. Now this mountainside town is thriving again as a tourist's haven for wine and art enthusiasts, history buffs, and ghost hunters.

As a testimony to one of my favorite movies, Field of Dreams, "if you build it…they will come," I created the most inviting space I could imagine, on a shoestring budget, and began the dream that will remain forever priceless. Throughout the past three years, I have been spoiled in the magic of thousands of soulful conversations with people from all over the world and many walks of life. I have had an incredible view to the obvious truth, as well as mind-blowing phenomena.

I still have a really hard time labeling myself as anything but me, just being me. Those who believe I am evil, practicing witchcraft and in need of saving, leave my presence with an enlightened understanding. Those who are initially skeptical, are quickly convinced I have a highly evolved level of intuitive awareness, as do they. The rest have immediately allowed the depth of my insight to validate their inner beauty and natural abilities. All are given a shot of love, an abundance of clarity and the path to personal empowerment: the best ground to launch a free spirit into flight.

Regardless of our pasts, we all hold the innate resources to be who we want to be, and to see our dreams come true; to bridge any internal gap of loneliness and discomfort with peace and acceptance; to give and receive unconditional love; to feel excitedly alive and appreciate our own worth; to know how to maintain happiness and a sense of well-being for the rest of our lives. Many, like me, have been aimlessly searching for the answers to our questions in other people, places or things.

This is a new kind of welcome basket of goodies; to all who are ready to be free, from all of us who have lived two worlds in one lifetime. You will be given a map to leave the land of illusion and the conformed who robotically sleep walk through each day, a light to show you the way to a heavenly garden of awakening, and a compass to keep you on the truest path to follow your bliss.

It is my deepest pleasure to coach you to greater awareness and empowerment, as you intuitively navigate through a full range of emotions which is your most accurate guidance. I am simply offering you a mirror of truth to reflect your strength and beauty within. Your best direction is to allow the highest version of you to create the rest of your story. It's time to fall in love with your own life, and gain the ultimate freedom to be you.

Welcome to Awakening! The possibilities of happy endings are infinite…

Chapter 1: The Catalysts to Transformation

I have often described my personal experience as being dropped into a foreign land with no guide, no map and no understanding of the language. After careful observation, I learned the way of life in that land and conformed to their standards. I hid behind the most appropriate masks and blended into the environment, just under the radar. Sadly, I never felt like I was truly at home, or with my own kind. In fact, the dream world of signs and symbols always made much more sense to me than being awake.

That is, until my Grandma Jo transitioned from this world to the next, and found her way back to me. At the time, I was still attempting to sleep my way through a life that I felt like I didn't belong in, and she was the perfect soul to fully wake me up. Not only was my Grandma my strongest anchor and shelter from any storm when she was alive, she was powerful enough to come back from the so called "dead," to help me want to live. The spirit of my Grandmother became my guide to Awakening and beyond.

Today, after 50 years on this planet, I have finally allowed my-self the freedom to be authentically me. After several decades of attempting to fit into a variety of disguises and directions to feel worthy and loved, I exhaustedly surrendered the sacrificial need to please. I released the requirement for any other's love, approval, or belief in me, and accepted only my own. What a freaking relief for everyone! By the way, no matter how much I evolve I can still cuss like a sailor; especially when I'm really passionate about what I'm saying.

I realize now, that I have been in the process of creating this message for many lifetimes; definitely before my birth here. When I started this book, over three years ago, I had no idea that I would be writing my way to full belief in me. My initial intention was to create a guide for anyone who wants to expe-rience true freedom in this lifetime, especially those who feel imprisoned by their own fear and disempowering thoughts. Much to my pleasant surprise, the first person to become the positive proof of this experiment was me.

Ironically, my neverending quest to determine the cause of my curse, turned out to be one of the greatest blessings I have ever been given: A highly evolved intuition, the strongest of all my senses. My torturous suffering was actually the powerful in-tensity of an unexplainable insight. The neverending search for the incredible mind who could help me, or the medicine that would make me feel better, ultimately led me to the awareness that I have a very special gift. The problem was, deep down, I was still hesitant to allow the full benefit of this ability in every area of my own life.

Despite the many years of research, resources, and education, the turning point was when I actually began listening to the information I was giving everyone else. I was coaching them on how to use the guidance of their intuition to lead the way forward. Every time I turned on the light for another, I found more of myself. I was already in direct contact with the wisdom of greater awareness, I just needed to stop looking outside of myself to find it.

You can imagine my shock and dismay as I began to unravel the many layers of conditioning only to uncover the same truth I always knew, but never allowed for myself. My healing could begin, and the incredible reprograming of my own mind, when I could feel the benefit of my own love from the inside out.

However, until I was able to walk into full belief and appreciation for me and my own life, I could always find strength and purpose in my love for other people. In fact, the depth of my love for them became the catalysts for my own transformations. The main motivation to keep moving forward came from my Grandma Jo, my sons, and the special few whom I respected, admired and trusted enough to allow the real me to be seen.

The day I was told my Grandma Jo was dying changed my life forever. I was 37, living in Phoenix, Arizona, and she was 87 in a hospital room in Iowa. Deep in a coma with her heartrate declining, the doctors gave her just a few hours to live so I didn't plan on getting to have a final conversation with her.

I packed my bags and grabbed the first flight I could get on. Soaring above the clouds, looking out at the city below getting smaller and smaller, I began to tearfully revisit the best memories of our time together. Lost in my own thoughts, I was startled back into the present when I heard someone call my name. I jerked my head around to see who it was, but observed only other passengers. As I settled back down in my seat, questioning my imagination, I heard my name again, "RENEE..." this time even louder and clearer. It was my Grandma's voice and I could suddenly feel her presence. I took the cue and silently asked her to please wait for me, unless she was ready to go.

On November 9, 2004 at approximately 11:20 pm, 12 hours after receiving the call and 20 minutes after reaching her side, my Grandma Jo slowly and peacefully drifted away. In her final breaths, I was holding her hand and telling her how much I loved her when I experienced something I still grasp to find words for. It was as if I could feel her spirit lift and move right through me.

I can only describe it as a gentle rush of blissful calm that completely consumed my entire being. I remember trying to explain to the rest of my grieving family, through my tears and exuberant wonderment, that I could feel her flying happy and free. To this day, the sensation of that memory has never left me.

Without a doubt, I knew it was her voice on the plane, just as she heard me from her bed, and waited for me to say goodbye. At the time, I really did believe that hospital room was our final farewell. Little did I know, the most amazing conversations between us had just begun.

Grandma Jo literally woke me up from my own self destruction. I know the only way I would have ever opened up to what was happening was because I already knew the energy of her spirit and I trusted her more than anyone. Through the power of love, my Grandma found a way to guide me out of my own hell, bringing the answers to my questions and helping me to understand finally who I am and why I came here.

During the very first visit, Grandma said she would tell me everything I wanted to know, but not all at once. She explained to me that I would remember our talks in bits and pieces as my mind could process and absorb the information. What I remember most, is when I asked her where she lived now she described it as the most beautiful dream you never want to wake up from, until you do.

The conversations with my deceased Grandma, definitely were the first of many wake up calls to get my attention. I knew then, without a shadow of a doubt, there is something much bigger going on here that what can be seen. It also validated why I have always been so fascinated in dreams and accurately interpreted them without ever studying how to. Now I see the signs, symbols, and synchronicities of daily situations and events, delivering the same message our dreams are giving us.

Each visit brought new insight to the reason that I always felt so freakishly abnormal. Grandma explained it as receiving invisible information which cannot always be proven in the physical world and therefore is non-existent to most humans. She said what seems so obvious to me is often never seen by others.

I get to see the highest and best version of everyone, as well as to understand how they think and feel about themselves right now. It also makes sense why my heartbreak and passion has always been for those who don't love themselves; I was automatically drawn to want to help those most like me. This is the work my soul chose to do here; but before I could truly help others, I would need to know how to heal myself first.

Grandma Jo has often reminded me of the sensation I felt when she left her body. She said it is the highest vibration of pure love; the true source of every human and the energy we will align with again. She said I am here to guide all who are lost and afraid how to move excitedly through life, and fearlessly transition to the afterlife.

I'm positive it was those conversations that gave me the strength to keep walking through my darkest days which were yet to come. The truest test came for me when I realized my worst fear was about to come true. My baby boy was showing signs of having the same poisonous energy running through him. Everything I had done to protect my sons from a world of addiction and madness was about to be busted wide open.

I was committed to do anything to walk my son through this; the bigger problem was that, deep down, I knew he had no intention of stopping. From the minute Quade was born I could see myself in his eyes. I knew he had the same uncomfortable nervous energy running through his body. He had an excruciating case of colic and cried more than cooed for the first three months of his life. Nothing could ever seem to soothe him.

Now as I sat with him in the emergency room, I could see no fear or regret anywhere in his eyes. For him, he had found an escape from his reality and a temporary place of relief for a while. It terrified me that he would experience the same torture, which almost destroyed me and several of my loved ones.

Of course, it was easy for me to take on the guilt and responsibility as the cause and the cure for my son's struggle. I believe this is a natural response for any parent whose child is experiencing addiction or any other self-destructive behavior. My every waking moment was filled with terror and panic in the thoughts of losing him. I put my life on hold. I stopped working, eating, sleeping, and even started losing my hair. I found no reason to laugh, to smile, or to take care of myself. I was dying and I didn't care. More days were spent in my bed with the covers over my head than I care to admit.

The deeper Quade went into his addiction, the deeper I went into my horror that I was losing him. I begged, I pleaded, I cried, I screamed; I was frantically running out of time and ideas. Nothing we were doing was having a lasting effect. He kept returning to the next dangerous drug that would take him away from us. The only time I felt peace is when he was in jail or on lock down in an institution. At least then I knew he was alive and safe.

Since I have always been the strongest one of anyone I know, I had very few people in my life who I could really lean on. I rarely confided in any of my family, friends or anyone else who had not survived the same nightmare. The last thing I needed were opinions, advice, or sympathy. I wanted solutions or nothing at all. I needed an army of angels and that's when it occurred to me, I already had access to them.

I decided to call on one of the souls who I had struggled with the most, my dad. He had died five years earlier, and most of our adult relationship was estranged. It was only during the last few weeks of his life that I truly got to connect with his soul again. I learned then just how amazing and magical the healing power of love is, especially in the face of death. It was as if our reality was encompassed in a bubble of light and nothing negative could enter.

In those final days with Dad, I was able to release an enormous amount of painful weight I had carried from the past. I knew he wanted us to have a better life than he had. I could feel how much he really loved us and that he would choose his own death if it meant getting his children back into his life, even if just for a few days. I was beginning to have understanding and compassion for the first man I ever loved and then hated. In a few days we were able to override years of hurt, sadness, and bitter resentments.

Now I was faced with reliving that hell again, and even worse, with my own son. One day, after receiving the call that Quade had left the latest rehab and was missing, I screamed out at the sky for my dad to help me. In a tearful and desperate plea, I told him if he wanted to make up for everything he had ever done to me, he would save my son. Once I could get my feelings under control again, I returned to work in hopes of getting lost in distraction for a while.

Seconds after I was seated at my desk, my personal printer started unexplainably printing page after page of meaningless letters, numbers and symbols. A coworker stopped by to jokingly ask me if I was printing a novel. I laughed and said I had not tried to print anything all day.

When it stopped, I pulled out the stack of papers and started flipping through the first few pages. I was quickly rendered speechless as one page instantly got my attention. It was completely blank except for one line at the top left that showed the letters "d#dadOX." I immediately knew my dad had heard me and I broke down, sobbing in shock and relief. Shortly after that, my son reached out for help after claiming to have heard a voice that led him to safety. I still have all of those pages, exactly as they printed out that day.

To this day, if I ever start to move into worry about Quade's path, I hold that vision as perfect validation of my dad's promise to me; to guide my son to safety. So far, I have only seen more and more evidence that he is still helping. I could finally let go of my need to save my child from himself, and release myself from my own pain and suffering, with love. In fact, as I write this, I can honestly say I have mastered the art of detached love, aka tough love, in response to my son's choices and consequences. It is never an easy thing to do, but it is absolutely possible.

My sons, Zach and Quade, were my only reason for living for a very long time. They were my motivation to keep moving forward and not to give up, even before they were born. I devoted my life to their wellbeing and the thought of losing either one of them was more than I could bear. I knew the best way to walk through my worst nightmare was to be the living proof of what's possible when you change your mind about your own reality.

Thus, regardless of all that I have survived so far, my experience as the mother of an addict has been the most painfully difficult, and always my best reason to continually evolve. My Grandma Jo opened me up to the ultimate power of love and infinite wisdom. It was now up to me to go beyond just being able to talk the talk and walk the walk; it was time for me to combine all worlds and live in the pure enjoyment of a blissful life.

I realize my story may be hard for many people to believe. Quite frankly, I had a hard time moving into complete belief of all of this myself. Once upon a time I was someone who had given up on life and was only functioning to bring joy to other people. My happily ever after could not truly begin until I applied what I knew, in order to fall in love with my own life... and this is how I did it.

Chapter 2: **How Life Works**

Honestly, I have no doubt that it has been my life's work, so far, just to understand how life works. If I had pursued degrees in the world of formal education, I'm certain I would have acquired at least one PhD by now. However, I was less concerned with the accolades of intelligence and credentials than I was determined to understand my own mind.

True to my rebellious free spirit, after graduating from high school, I refused to spend even one more second being taught information that I had absolutely no interest in learning. Instead, I built my own curriculum as a neverending seeker of knowledge and truth. I chose the books and any teachers with a hint of potential, to lead me to more than I already knew, especially about me. As the years went by, the underlying message was always the same: love yourself and you will be happy. As much as I completely agreed and pursued that objective, I could never quite get to the top of the mountain.

The impact of my Grandma Jo's grand entrance into my dreams was definitely enough proof for me to believe in something greater than what meets the eye. Without a shadow of a doubt, I now have complete knowledge that there is a very powerful source of infinite wisdom which we all have unlimited connection to. This is especially great news for the deepest thinkers, like me, who struggle to find other like-minded people to easily understand us. Until I was face to face with anyone who spoke my new language, I absorbed the communication from thousands of masters, healers, and scholars who did.

For me the most clarifying instruction about the human experience, which, in my opinion, truly encompasses all of the greatest teachings into one message, was when I was introduced to Esther Hicks and Abraham. I had just read the book and watched the movie, The Secret. Although I appreciated the awareness it was bringing to millions about the power of belief, I was looking for a much deeper explanation about the Law of Attraction than just how to manifest a car, a house, or a lover.

A few days later, I began reading yet another book by one of my favorite inspiring authors, Wayne Dyer. I typically researched anyone Dr. Dyer had made reference to when I was looking for something new to read or listen to. This time it was Esther Hicks, who is a channel for the non-physical group of greater intelligences called Abraham. I was hooked the minute I knew it was the same indisputable and empowering truth that applies to everyone and everything.

Ironically, even with the contact and communication with many of my own transitioned loved ones, I was still skeptical of those humans who claimed to do the same thing. Much to my joyful surprise, when I aligned these law-based teachings with my own proven experience, as well as the insight I was getting from beyond the physical, I finally had the answers to my questions so far.

For me, understanding the Law of Attraction (meaning that which is likened to itself is drawn, or like energy attracts like energy) was a mind-blowing awareness of exactly how life works for the benefit of all. In fact, it validated everything I somehow always knew but kept resisting. After almost 10 years, Esther and Abraham are still my preferred guidance to revisit; especially when I'm out of sync.

Frankly, there has already been so much written and discussed on the subject of the Law of Attraction, that I don't feel the need to keep repeating the same universal wisdom. However, because I personally know the priceless pay off of this inside information, I want to share the basic principles of abundance and wellbeing as the perfect place to start. If I can inspire even one person to fall more in love with life, through my own testimonial or any others, then it was all worth it.

As one of the most stubbornly resistant persons on the planet, it took undeniable evidence and eye-opening phenomena, to slap me in the face before I could even look in the right direction. Eventually I would love to see all Universal Laws to be recognized as an important part of the information we teach to small children. If I have my way, everyone will understand how to leverage the power of the Universe from within.

For now, I'm offering a crash course in the game of life. The sooner you understand the rules and implement a working strategy, the sooner you will be free to experience a reality that matches your dreams. The first thing you need to remember?

The ultimate authority of your human experience is always YOU. By the way, this is what the happiest, healthiest and wealthiest people on the planet already know and live by.

There are basically two parts to every human. The biggest part is the soul; also known as spirit/love/higher self. The other part is the physical version of us, a one-of-a-kind individual with a mind, emotions, and a body. Your spirit is the energy of pure love, being temporarily housed in a physical body.

You were given a brain to reason with as you explore and expand beyond previous boundaries. You were given a sensory system to accurately navigate your way through this environment and keep you on track. You were given intuition so you can continually connect with the truth of your soul/source, always guiding you with love. You are a spiritual being having a human experience; coexisting with other playmates who are also creating their own reality. Play nice and have fun!

The bottom line is, you are the only one creating your own reality. You are the starting point for everything and everyone you are attracting into your life. You will never get it all done, and it's not your job to save or change the world. There is nothing broken that you need to fix.

Many people have a hard time with this truth because we don't want to believe we would deliberately create anything bad for ourselves. Especially if we are currently struggling, or believe that something is inherently wrong with us, or with the rest of civilization. Nevertheless, the sooner you take ownership for your own life, the sooner you have the power to create worlds.

Again and again many of us have played the role of helpless victim, with a weakened mind that's convinced we have no choice. We feel powerless to feel better about "that" subject, until "that" condition changes. We are waiting for prayers to be answered and outside situations to be corrected before we can truly be happy and free. We are lost in the illusion that life is about luck, fate, coincidence, and the fortunately blessed or unfortunately cursed.

One of the biggest misconceptions out there is that life is randomly throwing things at you to deal with, or learn lessons from, when it's actually just responding to your own strongest beliefs about yourself, and your expectations of life. Through the Law of Attraction, what you truly believe, is what you will receive; what you expect, is what you will get. You are absolutely setting up your own future with the dominant thoughts you are thinking right now; especially about yourself.

Sadly, there are still far too many of us who live life by default; working hard to hold our heads above water while preparing for the next wave of problems or worries to hit. Unknowingly, we have been trained to believe that we have very little say in our own experience.

This is mainly because so many of us have been taught to follow a "superior" (an older, smarter, more experienced person): our parents, teachers, bosses, preachers, government, etc. We are encouraged to follow an outside authority, rather than listening to the truth of our highest self. Therefore, the bulk of humanity has a habitual tendency to blindly follow the leader with the loudest voice.

News flash! We are not here to be clones of each other, no matter how much genetics or brainwashing come into play. Nor are we here to get everyone to think, speak, or act in exactly the same way; all in an effort to validate our own beliefs. In fact, if this were truly the case, what would be the purpose of being here?

Rather than spinning in the delusion of getting all minds to unite in one belief system, why not start with the undeniable truths that apply to the entire human race? No matter the details of our personal story, from the moment we take our first breath, to our last breath, we are all part of the same perfect process. We are born into an environment, which aligns perfectly with our own sensory perception, just like animals and other living creatures on the planet, allowing us to use our natural instincts to navigate through the unknowns of every new day.

Without a contrasting environment, known as the Law of Duality, life would be a meaningless existence; not to mention robotically mind-numbing. We need night to know day, light to know darkness, and the differences between us to know ourselves. Even siblings born of the same parents, raised exactly the same way, will have an individual perspective about their childhood and of who they think they are. This is why we were each given a brain, to think for ourselves.

Every person is built with the same guidance system, your emotions. How you feel is instant communication if you're thinking is in a direction that is positive or negative for you. So, rather than attempt the impossible task of monitoring and analyzing the validity of your thoughts, just notice what you are feeling when you think them. Committing to emotional wellbeing as your top priority is the starting point to health, happiness, and unlimited abundance in this physical dimension. The circumstances of your life, will always match the overall mindset you operate from; every time, no exceptions.

Why is it so important to understand your mind and emotions in connection with how life works? Because this IS how your life works. Your environment, and everything in it, is vibrational energy, including your thoughts. What you give your full attention to, sends a signal to the universal mind through the Law of Attraction which is continually bringing new experiences that match your strongest beliefs right now.

In the least amount of words, you create your reality with your own mind.

If you are caught up in worries and doubts, you will be given more opportunities to work through your fears. If you are in a state of appreciation and knowing it's all good no matter what, you will see everything working out well for you. Most people still have no clue that any of this is happening behind the scenes, and yet this information is the quickest route to happiness and personal empowerment.

Please understand clearly, none of this has anything to do with human laws created to govern a society which are basically a means to control each other. The basis for most rules and requirements, placed on imperfect people by imperfect people, is mostly about fostering fear of punishment for disobedience. Human based laws are inconsistent, imperfect, and up for debate depending on who's in charge.

For that matter, this isn't about judgement of winners and losers, right and wrong, or good and bad. There is a ridiculous amount of time and money spent on the neverending task of protecting law-abiding citizens from criminals. Here's a thought, rather than building more prisons, why not teach our youth how to positively manage their minds and emotions to begin with?!

Universal laws are eternal and all inclusive, operating in perfect harmony for all of creation. This is the way of nature and the fundamental principles that apply to the entire universe and everything in it. These rules are easy to follow because there is nothing we really have to do except keep ourselves in positive alignment with the truest source energy of our wellbeing: love. You don't even need to be aware of any of this in order to receive the benefit.

What you do need to know is, there is nothing and no one outside of you, who can force you to think a certain way. Nor is it possible to be ruled by subconscious thoughts that you have no control over. Only your active thoughts have vibrational influence. If you are having an emotional reaction, positive or negative, the preceding momentum of aligned thoughts is the only originating source you need to be aware of.

Instead of living in fear of the future, or regretting your past, embrace the adventure of the present moment! Allow yourself the endless buffet and assortment of treats this dimension has to offer you. From beginning to end, all you really need to do is follow the path of least resistance, which is the direction that you feel the most clarity about right now. Learning to trust yourself and practice feeling good along the way will allow you to have more fun as you grow and continue moving forward.

An awareness and application of the universal laws will help you leverage full enjoyment of your human experience as well as save you an enormous amount of time from being lost in confusion. The Law of Attraction, also known as the Law of Love, is the managing energy we use to create and coexist in. The sooner you go with this flow, the easier you will float down the natural stream of amazing connections with other people.

I like to imagine my highest guide as an all-inclusive and loving observer; the parental mastermind of greater consciousness, at the highest level of awareness, operating an entire human race, through a vibrational frequency of unconditional love. It is so perfect and pure that it is impossible to see, hear, taste, touch or smell, yet this potion of passion can breathe life into any of the physical senses and sensations. The same powerful energy that creates everything and everyone is also set up to help us temporarily survive and thrive in this galaxy.

From this viewpoint, humanity is basically just one enormous family. With an infinite number of members evolving at their own pace, through a variety of experiences. They are inspired to new thoughts and desires with each new generation which impacts and elevates future generations and how we relate to each other along the way. Ultimately we reach the level of un-conditional love for all souls, in complete self-awareness that we are all part of one divine love and neverending.

I realize there are many names given to the all that is, yet nameless: God, Buddha, Tao, Universe, Source, Higher Power, and so on. I'm not here to debate the words a group of people uses to define or explain their belief system, with regard to an ultimate entity. However, I do want to shine a light on the power you hold within your own belief of yourself.

Each one of us believes and perceives based on our own experiences up to this point. What is true for one, is not always true for another. Quite honestly, a belief is just a combination of similar thoughts that we think. Eventually this combination becomes our truth. It is often firmly planted by our family trees and passed down without anyone ever questioning its current value or validity.

Nothing is written in stone. Whatever you believe is true in the current moment, can change at any point if you decide it no longer serves your highest and best interest. However, it is pointless, not to mention that it can literally drive you insane, to go to battle with your thoughts in order to receive clarity. When you focus on the relief of feeling better first, you can clear out a lot of the mental chaos and confusion.

Fortunately, your emotions are the perfect compass to identify your current direction of thought. How you feel in the present is the best indication: if you are focusing on what you want or the opposite of what you want. It seems like a very fine line but the feeling is extremely different. Simplified, if you feel like crap, you have been feeding yourself a load of shit. If you feel great, your mind is aligned with the true source within you, pure love.

Your emotions give you immediate insight to manage your ever expanding mind. Although negative emotion gets a bad rap, it is actually a necessary part of your internal navigation system in this universe. An uncomfortable feeling is often the only thing that will get your attention. It keeps you safe and healthy, and it motivates you to create your own solutions for what you identify as problems.

Experiencing emotions such as hurt, sadness, anger, fear, and others does not mean you are failing, falling, or taking steps backward. The key is to examine the emotion for the clarity and awareness it can offer. Then do your absolute best to redirect your thinking to the best feeling thoughts available and believable to you right now.

I am a tried and true advocate of any form of meditation over any form of medication, whether lying in your bed, or being one with nature, or even just simply taking a few deep, cleansing breaths. By far these are the quickest and most beneficial ways to clear your mind and calm your emotions. Anytime you become aware of when you are feeling upbeat and all is well, make a mental note of the reasons or thoughts behind it. This is the proven data you can return to, when you are in a less than positive mindset.

Universal intelligence will never override self-will, but will work in perfect partnership with you, always in agreement with whatever you choose next. How do you know if you are on the right path? By observing your own happiness and satisfaction right now.

Are you seeing more issues than opportunities, pushing and pulling yourself through your days? Or are you easily moving through life and love, more often than not enjoying what you are creating, and excited to experience more? Believe it or not, everything is a whole lot easier and a lot more fun when you stop making life harder than it actually is.

Do you want more harmonious relationships? Rewarding work doing what you love? Financial abundance? Perfect health? The freedom to be yourself at all times? Or perhaps you are seeking a deeper connection to a love beyond any other experience you have ever known? The only thing that will block you from seeing and feeling every experience you desire, is your own doubt and disbelief that it will happen. Keep looking in the direction of full belief and good feeling energy.

Honestly, what you say and what you do have very little significance in determining your ultimate outcomes. The universe hears the vibrational voice of your deepest belief, not your words or actions. It is so much more efficient and beneficial to get very clear and intentional within before you respond to another or take action on any major decisions.

This insight is very simple yet empowering because now you have complete control over your own happiness. Let go of the impossible mission of trying to outsmart universal truth, endlessly searching for a detour to bypass the emotional process of transformation. Ultimately, this route will never offer the deep satisfaction that developing your mind to positive belief and trusting your own intuition will bring.

The true secret to a happy life is not discovered just from the knowledge of how life works for others, but in the continual development of your highest self from the insight you are receiving and resonating with. Knowledge without implementation is just knowledge. Words alone do not teach, your own experience does.

Do you need more persuading why taking responsibility for everything happening in your own life is good advice? For starters, if you are the one who is in charge of bringing every experience to yourself, then you are also the one that has the power to create new experiences. You no longer have to wait for someone to change, or a condition to improve, before you can be happy. You get to have fun right now and everything else will line up with that energy for as long as you stay in a mindset of empowerment and full belief.

Many people are hard at work focused on the best action plan to create wealth, health, love, and happiness, typically regretting mistakes in the past or fearful of the unknown future. Fewer people are really aware of their incredible ability to manifest within their own mind. Even fewer will live in positive alignment with universal truth and allow everything to come to them with the most natural timing and order, effortlessly flowing through them, and to them.

Our possibilities are unlimited; our path is certain yet joyously unknown; we already have everything we need to create the most magical human experience we could ever imagine. There is only a source of wellbeing that you are allowing or not. You will feel the positive or negative effect of staying in the flow. All we need to do is keep moving in the direction that aligns with our idea of our highest self, all else will fall perfectly in place around us.

Life is an exciting and emotional journey forward. There is no need to go back and right the wrongs of yesterday. The best starting point is where you are right now. You will learn how to positively manage your mind, and you learn to care more about how you feel, and trust your intuition as you walk through each day.

As someone who leaned toward suicide for the better part of 40 years, I have found that it is absolutely possible to have a peaceful bliss in this lifetime, especially for those most tortured by their own brilliant minds and kind hearts. No longer will you just function through your days, never truly falling in love with your own life. It's time for you to be free while you're still alive. What do you have to lose except a mind that is treating you like your worst enemy?

As we venture through the next chapters, I will offer several examples of how the Law of Attraction applies to every aspect of life. You can pick and choose the processes and tools that work best for you. I encourage anything and everything that resonates with what you feel to be true for you and in your best interest. Anything you incorporate should feel like a positive experience to enhance your day, not just rituals and routines to check off the list. More will be revealed and discovered from a connective point of attraction.

If you can embrace and practice these fundamental truths, in every aspect of your life, you will absolutely achieve whatever you envision. More importantly, you will know how to be happy no matter what. This entire process can be narrowed down to three steps but will take as much time and experiences as needed for each soul to embrace these principles from the inside out. Those who do will inevitably experience total freedom in the human experience.

- Understand and accept the basic, natural laws of the universe at work for everyone; especially the Law of Attraction or Law of Love.

- Practice this new found wisdom in everything you do and apply to every area of your life.

- Allow the flow of loving, abundant energy to come to you and through you at all times.

Chapter 3: More Questions than Answers

Many people, including myself, have been experiencing the opposite of what we really want for most of our lives. There are hidden wounds and deep seated emotions attached to our history, within each one of us. The past often becomes the story we tell to explain who we are today.

If you can imagine the stages of your life as the chapters of a book or scenes in a movie, you can better visualize the details of your story up to this point. Who you think you are and how you see the world is just your current story line and is always changing to keep things interesting. The role you choose to play most is the character you will most likely be known for.

In the beginning, we are born to circumstances that become the basis of our story, or so we think. We will either adapt to the belief systems of our genealogy, society, government, culture, peers, friends, and loved ones as we create our ever expanding roles or we will resist them. Our leading role is based on the details we believe to be true about past events, as well as who we want to be in the future.

As we add in the dynamics of relating to other people, we add multiple levels of conditions, expectations, and obligations. Eventually we will discover that everyone around us is simply a reflection of ourselves in different mirrors always demonstrating the full range between what we love and what we fear. Each individual is having their own positive or negative experience, even in relationships with one another. No one is right or wrong, good or bad, nor is anyone to blame.

It is that last sentence that seems to cause humans the most grief. We falsely believe it would be a better place if everyone was more like us, especially those we love most. We secretly wish people would just agree to think, feel, react and understand from our perspective and, preferably, at all times. This is obviously an impossibility and can destroy many relationships in the process of trying to make it happen. We are in a world of variety on purpose. The truth is that the differences between us offer the greatest clarity about ourselves.

Allow me to offer a common experience that you will most likely find yourself in at one time or another during this human experience. You'll have a loved one, or several, who negatively consumes your waking thoughts (or maybe the loved one is you). You desperately want to understand and change the circumstance or situation that they continually find themselves in, whatever that may be.

Regardless of the particular concern or fear that plagues us about another, or ourselves, the question we always ask is "WHY?" Why would someone so smart and talented use drugs and alcohol to escape their reality? Why would someone who seems to "have it all" be depressed and even suicidal?

Why would someone not have the desire to make their health and well-being and/or their minor children, top priority? Why would someone stay in a relationship/marriage that continually leaves them feeling trapped, neglected, betrayed, or abused? Why does someone so obviously amazing to everyone else, not see it for themselves?

The answer is the same for all of the questions above. You are observing someone who doesn't have a true sense of their own worth and purpose. They offer very little love and appreciation to themselves, if any.

Here are the facts. No one is susceptible to a life of addiction unless they are looking for a complete escape from reality. No one ends their life unless they are sick and tired of the human experience. No one deliberately hurts themself, or another living being, from a place of self-love. This does not excuse or justify any unhealthy behaviors, but it does give insight into why people do what they do.

I will give you another typical scenario. You talk to someone you care about who goes on and on about every concern they may have, either right now, in the past, or in the future. You feel bad for this person because they do seem to have their unfair share of rotten luck or difficult challenges and plenty of terrible things to feel awful about. You sympathize, you encourage, you offer solutions, and in the end you are both left with the same conclusion left in your minds: life has not been kind to this person.

The truth is, our loved one is caught in a vicious cycle of self-destructive thinking. They respond to life's ups and downs with the same historical level of feeling helpless and hopeless. Con-

39

tinually waiting for someone or something to make it better, oblivious to the fact that they are the one actually creating all of it and unknowingly asking for more of the same.

These are the people we wish we could be completely honest with but are afraid it will only add more salt to their wounds. Instead, we let them go on and complain, blame, and excuse their plight. We simply nod in agreement and offer compassion (along with many other not so compassionate thoughts and emotions) and finally our prayers. Eventually, we avoid spending time with them because we are left feeling mentally and emotionally drained when we do.

Most people feel that it is a good thing to let someone continue to talk about their problems. After all, isn't that what a good person does? Listen as we offer sympathy and any amount of hope we can muster? Maybe our loved one is just lonely and in need of someone to talk to. Or possibly, we think that this time we will say the magic words that will help them see the light. There is also a high likelihood that focusing on the troubles of another's life, is a welcome distraction to help us leave our own for a while.

No matter what your true intentions are, it is never helpful to anyone to give more attention to anything unwanted. In fact, when you add your emotional energy to the problems of another, you are actually adding fuel to their fire. The most loving thing you can do for your loved ones is to be a living example of complete wellbeing. You are of no real service to anyone unless you are overflowing with the positive knowing and empowerment from your own experiences.

More answers will be revealed in the coming chapters of this book. For now, keep an open and compassionate heart as we take a closer look at other people, ourselves, and the experiences that shape our lives. You will begin to see the connection between what you ask for, what you truly believe, and what is manifested as a result. It's time to get to the bottom of the underlying belief systems that are holding you back from the rest of your life, so you might want to take some notes.

Chapter 4: **Clearing out the Crap**

So, you made it this far! Congratulations on your commitment to yourself! It really does take a deep level of dedication to take this internal journey to an unknown world. I know you already have what it takes or you wouldn't be reading this book. Please give yourself all of the love, patience, and encouragement needed to heal. There may be buried pain, and fear-based beliefs, which rise to the surface as you process through the information you are absorbing and practicing. (Now would be a good time to grab a journal or notebook to write down any defining milestones or lightbulb moments.)

The only time I feel it is beneficial to revisit even an ounce of pain from the past, is in order to gain insight to any blocks in the present. The goal is to release as much negative energy as possible as the best way to completely recover and move forward. Without question, any old wounds that still need healing will remain a sore spot until we release the power they hold to make us bleed.

We are going to start by getting to a place and time in your mind that you can remember as one of the longest stretches of doing well and feeling great. It could be as recent as yesterday or maybe it was your childhood. Possibly it was the thrill of leaving home to conquer the world or landing your dream job. For some, it was finding the love of your life and starting a family, or maybe it was being footloose and fancy free to be and do whatever you wanted. Whatever period of time it was when you felt on top of the world and everything just seemed to line up perfectly and effortlessly, is the time to refer to.

Let's take a deeper look at what was really happening during those joyous times that hold such dear memories you can never forget them. Contrary to popular belief, the experiences and events that stand out as the happiest, most positive, and offer a long lasting appreciation, were not a matter of coincidence, luck, fate, or privilege. You may have had help, but you created all of it by staying true to your vision with full belief.

You kept your eye on the prize instead of allowing doubt and worry to block you from it. You were enjoying the ride to the destination, not whining and complaining that you were not there yet, or afraid that someone might beat you to it. You were in perfect vibrational alignment with the positive, loving flow of universal energy—the Law of Attraction. You weren't over thinking and resisting, you just allowed and enjoyed.

Now remember a time that really stands out when everything just seemed to suck. Perhaps you lost a job or other income that led to financial strain and stress. Maybe it was a health issue, life stressor, or a crisis of a loved one. Possibly it was a death or the end of a relationship that you thought would last a lifetime.

Any past events that jump out for you, are the ones you can gain the most clarity from. (Another good time to write in your journal and note the dominant emotion when you think of it.)

What was actually happening during those times in your life, those times that can easily be identified as the most difficult for you, are the exact catalysts that show you your own strength and coping skills, if you allow them to. Endings are painful when you are emotionally attached to specific outcomes, or people, never changing. The suffering in the human experience happens anytime we get stuck in the idea of permanence. When you stay loyal to sadness, fear, anger, or hurt, you will delay feeling better for as long as you deem necessary.

Have you ever experienced the domino effect of when it rains, it pours or Murphy's Law? That is really just the Law of Attraction in action. It's not that you intentionally sit around thinking about negative things that you want to happen. On the contrary, most people think about those things because they are trying to avoid them.

However, the law of attraction doesn't work on the premise of distinguishing what you want over what you don't want. The universe says yes to everything you give your dominant attention and emotional energy to. It returns similar vibrational experiences and evidence like a boomerang, no exceptions.

Does that mean if you worry about your loved ones' health or safety, something is going to happen to them? No, since everyone has self-will and is in charge of their own reality. However, any worry and fear you are continually funneling through your own body will eventually threaten your own wellbeing.

Acknowledging your preferences is a very natural thing to do and in fact is a necessary part of the human experience. How would you ever know what you prefer without experiencing variations of the opposite? If you didn't get somewhat emotionally attached to people, places, and things you love, you would never really know the full benefit of loving.

The key is to refrain from getting so caught up in the need for something, or someone, to be different before you can feel better. When you wait for everything to improve before you can relax, you will never be at peace. Many are so caught up in the details of a busy life and setting up their future, that they are missing out on the joy of the ride.

The silent observer within, our objective self, always knows that this time and space is temporary. Our only real comfort is to continually love ourselves through anything that comes our way, creating as much fun and adventure with others along the way.

Is there anything you still hold on to? What is it that you thought you had come to terms with, only to find it creeping in again and again? What is it that continues to kick your ass? No matter who or what was the cause of the injury, pain is pain, and it will only stay alive for as long as you continue to breathe life into it. For your spirit to truly be free, it is necessary to allow the memories of your past to have a safe and loving energy to dissolve into. (It is a good time to write about who or what event you feel is holding you back from the rest of your life, the most present and obvious is the best place to start.)

I completely understand the compelling reasons and desire to believe that your problems are someone else's fault. We want to believe that if certain things had not happened, or did happen, we would be happier and have a better life. However, latching on to these powerless beliefs will only leave us feeling that an event or another person has ruined our opportunity to see anything differently. This just isn't true, not for you or anyone else. There are no lost chances, nothing to regret, no one to blame (including ourselves), except what we believe in our own mind.

Frankly, it was just too easy to blame my dad for all of my issues. After all, my first memory is the feeling of fear and helplessness. I can remember pulling myself up and barely peeking over the top of my crib, as I watched my dad hit my mom until she cried and begged him to stop. My weekends were more like those of a wounded soldier surviving a war zone, than a few days of downtime having fun being a kid. Instead of choosing a family time activity, my siblings and I were deciding who would have the courage to jump into the middle of the fight, and possibly take the hit—or run to the neighbors and call the police.

As the oldest, I was usually the one who took on the brunt of the dysfunction. I was punished for anything my younger brother and sister did wrong, for taking my mom's side in their battles, and any time I spoke the truth about my dad. When I did, he would force me to sit in front of him for hours at a time as he unleashed his rage. He called me every name in the book and convinced me I had nothing to offer anyone. The only way he would stop was if I agreed with every horrible thing he was saying about me and everyone I loved. Alcohol took the blame as the monster feeding his madness, but I always knew there had to be much bigger demons he was fighting.

For the first 15 years of my life, until Mom and Dad were divorced, I had a front row seat to the cycle of domestic violence, addiction, and abuse. The final straw for me was the night when I truly believed he was going to kill my mom. Their battle had moved into the bathroom where I could hear my dad attempting to drown my mom in the bathtub.

Fueled by pure terror and adrenalin, I charged at him like a wild animal and pulled him off her. He turned his wrath on me and threw me against the wall like a rag doll. I will never forget the horror in his eyes when he realized what he had done, or the vindication I felt, knowing my mom would never allow him to hurt us again.

No matter how deep the wound, it is always the right time to allow a final cleansing so healing can take place. The ego/human self will always hide, protect, and defend any of our old issues that have yet to be addressed. The spirit/higher self will always serve as the best healer.

Express whatever feelings and words you need to have about a certain person and/or event, in order to move forward in the direction that feels better and better. Putting the pains of your past to rest will truly change your life. The harsh reality is when you hold on to the negative energy of what was done by another, or done by you, you will only imprison yourself in a life of misery, and the possibility of an early grave.

Many people are afraid that if they release the anger and resentment they feel completely justified in having, this will in some way give a stamp of approval to what happened. However, the only person we are truly punishing by holding in all of that poison, is ourselves. We cannot wish harm to another without harming ourselves. Nor can we ever truly be happy while at the same time wishing for bad things to happen to another regardless of what they have done. Be selfish enough to release blame and guilt. Allow yourself the freedom to feel good again.

There is no one in this universe that is perfect. Everyone can get lost, confused, and conflicted. Everyone can say and do things that are hurtful to themselves and to others. Whether intentional or unintentional, all humans are capable of anything and everything. Regardless of the injustice, no one ever wins through the eyes of hate and revenge. Those who choose to lash out against society have become disconnected from their own source of love.

Holding on to negative bitterness will only take you down in the process. If you are filled up with excuses, rationalizations, and justification of why you think and feel the way you do, there is not much room left for anything else. You literally block peace, love, and abundance from flowing freely through you, and to you. Deliberately fueling the fire of pain will only keep you trapped in it. Therefore, you are punishing no one other than yourself.

If you want to evolve, you must let go of your ego's need to be right. When you release the chains that keep you bound to the troubles of yesterday, your soul is free to soar into infinite possibilities. Your focus must always stay on your ultimate wellbeing.

You will not heal from a place of blame or guilt; you will not heal from a place of anger and resentment; you will not heal from a place of judging good and bad, right and wrong, nor from a place of feeling fear and unworthiness. You will heal with the energy of a positive mindset, allowing love and compassion for yourself and everyone else.

Have you ever read or heard an inspiring story that didn't include some sort of huge challenge or hardships to overcome? True spiritual development evolves from the wake up calls and life events that, initially, we may consider to be a mistake, crisis, disaster, tragedy, or trauma. These are the crucial hours that truly show us what we're made of, and eventually will be recognized as the catalysts of our transformation.

Each experience that comes into your reality is happening on purpose and in response to your truest intentions and desires. The clearer you are about what you really want, the greater the resonance you will feel when it shows up. It could be as simple as something that brings a smile to your face, or it could be the incredible mate who lights your fire. Everything is happening by universal timing and will match the frequency and momentum of what you are a vibrational match to.

You are ultimately the only one who is creating your own outcome in any situation. No other person truly has power over you unless you believe they do—not your boss, not the government, not your spouse/partner, not your parents, not your children, not your family, nor your friends. You are the one that chooses your own response and reality. You decide your own positive or negative reaction in every moment. Even the weakest and most vulnerable among us has free will to believe what they want to believe.

You have heard the blanket messages your entire life. You hold the answers within, you cannot love anyone if you don't love yourself first, you can be your best friend or your worst ene-my; trust yourself and stay true to yourself above all else. You can logically comprehend exactly what they mean and even believe that the same thing is true for everyone. However, if you have not made the internal commitment to actively apply this truth to every part of your life, then you are truly missing out on just how incredibly amazing you really are.

So what prevents you from doing this? I hear so many reasons in the work I do with other people, not to mention the book of excuses I wrote for myself. Here goes…. I don't have enough time to do what I want because I'm too busy taking care of everyone else; If (fill in the blank), would happen, then I could be, do, have, what makes me happy; I don't even know what I want; I have people dependent on me and their needs come first; I don't have the money to do what I want; I don't have a partner who believes in me and supports me; I don't have the confidence to do what I want; I have too many issues to ever be completely free and happy; If I didn't have this disease, handicap, disability, (fill in the blank), I could have, be, do, what I want.

If you are cautiously living a life based on what you fear, you will always find a reason that prevents your happiness. If you want to live a life based on what you love, you will make the best of whatever challenges and obstacles you are presented with. You can treat every situation as a reason to fail or as the inspiration to help you fly higher. Which life feels better to you?

I know firsthand how hard all of this can be to accept and take ownership of my own life. It was difficult for me to believe that I had created the experience of becoming a struggling single mom, as I was losing my income. Around 2007, when the real estate/financial bubble burst, I was working for a mortgage company in Phoenix, Arizona and it was one of the first impacted by the crash.

I became financially, emotionally, and mentally bankrupt. I lost my home and many material possessions. I even lost friends and family, but worst of all, I lost the belief that I could ever have an amazing life of my own creation.

I tried to blame my ex-husband and past relationships; I tried to blame my employers; I tried to blame the government and the greed of the wealthy; I tried to blame my parents and past experiences that, I believed, set me up to fail from the beginning. The truth is, I was living way beyond my means and already struggling to maintain a lifestyle that could only offer a temporary escape from the miserable thoughts and feelings I had about myself.

I wanted to create the appearance of a perfect life in hopes that I would one day believe it too. No matter what I achieved on the outside of me, deep down I always knew the truth; I had no idea who I was, or even what I wanted anymore. I was living a life built on the belief that there was something wrong with me and I just needed to find a way to be normal. The opinion of strangers mattered more than my own and I easily became the person anyone needed me to be, in order to be accepted.

All of this did not happen because of a traumatic childhood or because I became a single mom or because I lost my job. My life was continually showing me the proof of what I believed about myself from a very young age. I was choosing to stay loyal to an old belief system that was destroying me.

I was loyal to the belief that love means you cannot be happy unless everyone you love is happy. I still heard the devastated child who reminded me not to get too excited about anything so it wouldn't hurt when it was taken away. I bought into the mentality that I would have to struggle and sacrifice for anything I wanted. I was struck with the powerless and paralyzing reality of believing I didn't even have the choice to change my own mind, let alone my entire life.

I share all of this as an example of what your deepest beliefs will ultimately create in your reality. What I believed about myself was showing up in every area of my life. It affected my health, my relationships, my work and, my spirit. I had to change my mind in order to change my life. There was no amount of money or love outside of me that could offer the acceptance of me. I had to go to the deepest level of healing I could go to, a place of complete surrender and knowing that I was ready to embrace the demons I was running from.

If you feel you need more hands-on help right now, there are numerous avenues for support and guidance in your local communities. I spent most of my life seeking assistance outside of myself, and I will always encourage the most natural and simple avenues to relief. It is ultimately about quality of life and you are the only authority who can decide what that means for you. No matter the degree of dysfunction, disease, or diagnosis you may be currently identifying with, you have the ability to gradually transform any negative condition, into a positive direction—whenever you are ready.

In order to create the most magical and exciting life ever, you must allow the expansion and/or replacement of your own limiting belief system. You must release any resistance to who you are naturally. You must learn to let go of the crap that keeps you stuck in a fearful and negative reality, blocking your spirit from truly being free to soar to new and breathtaking heights.

Chapter 5: **Unpacking Your Relationship Baggage**

In the millions of conversations I have had with other people, regardless whether I was hearing from a stranger or someone I had known my whole life, one area continues to baffle people the most; romantic relationships. The individual's age, gender, education, or occupation doesn't matter, there is still far more confusion about love and intimacy, than clarity. The difficulty lies in the belief system of the individual who is asking. I have the extreme pleasure of letting everyone in on the best-kept secret in order to attract amazing love into their lives.

Fortunately, and also unfortunately, I am someone who has accepted that I can intuitively see beyond the details and superficial appearance. It also means I have a front row seat to the truth behind the closed doors, as well as every closet full of skeletons. In story after story, and in every stage of a relationship, there is predominantly one thing that will inevitably ruin the best of friendships, long time partners, and romantic connections: FEAR.

Fear of intimacy, fear of getting hurt, fear of loss, fear of rejection, fear of losing control, fear of losing self, fear of abandonment, fear of being inadequate, fear of being unlovable or unworthy of love, fear of truth and consequences, fear of failure, fear of …(fill in your own blank).

After hearing from a variety of happy couples, those mending from a broken heart, as well as knowing the truth of my own experiences, it is easy to see how so many people can be stunned and shaken when it comes to intimacy in relationships. The reality is that most people have very little concept of how to manage their own mind and emotions, let alone how to navigate through the thoughts and feelings of another person. Add in the dynamics of personal history, sex, work, family, finances, and so on, and you incorporate several more layers of unknown to comprehend.

My goal is not to debate lifestyle, marital status, sexual needs and preferences, whether or not to have children, parenting, or any other major decisions that are healthy and appropriate for you. I completely understand how important and sensitive these issues are to the entire planet, and that is why there are already numerous books and teachings on these subjects. My soul's intention is to offer clarity and insight about your previous patterns, and current conditions, for those who are ready to create deeper connections and authentic intimacy, whether you choose to "formally" join your life with someone or not.

The Wardrobe of Conformity

From the moment we take our first breath, we are infused with the energy of other people's ideas, especially about love and re-lationships and the human experience. As babies and toddlers, we are in complete alignment with our own truth and natural tendencies. As we begin to adapt more to our caretakers, and immediate surroundings, we start to seek the approval and acceptance of others. Digesting a mixture of verbal messages, visual images, and positive or negative emotional vibrations, these messages become part of our foundation in what we be-lieve a good/bad child, parent, friend, and partner is.

As you mature, and become more independent and obser-vantly aware, you are really the only one who can decide what love means for you now, especially as you spend time relating with other people. All of your encounters are created from new inputs, as a result of the love and loss you have experienced along the way.

Granted, some relationships are easier to navigate through than others, but all of them have important information to offer you. The people you deeply care about can inspire your greatest joy as well as your deepest sorrow. In fact, an abundant range of emotions can be attributed simply from your attachment and expectations of those you love most.

Notice I said, from your attachment and expectations of those you love most. Whenever you completely link your sense of wellbeing and happiness to another person, you also give them an enormous power over you. Whether it's a child or parent, a family member or dear friend, a current lover, or former part-ner, you will always experience greater joy and successful interactions, when you can allow everyone the freedom of unconditional love.

In the same respect, the sooner you can learn to emotionally detach from others' opinions and acceptance of you, the happier you will be. When you catch yourself in too much worry, fear, sadness, hurt, anger, rejection, or guilt, do everyone a favor and take some time to chill out. As you learn to be less concerned about what everyone else is thinking and doing, and more focused on positive alignment within yourself, you will have access to instant relief.

Contrary to popular opinion, it is not your loved one's job, or even humanly possible, to remain consistently focused on your happiness above their own. Nor is it the highest love to devote more of your time and attention to others, while neglecting yourself. Prioritizing a loved one's comfort and wellbeing above your own is neither an empowering way to live, nor to lead with. The longer you remain in the cycle of seeking your joy and greater purpose through another, the longer you miss out on the most amazing part of yourself.

To be honest, there will always be a certain amount of attachment to other humans. Without it, you would not know and appreciate the truest value in the gift of life. However, when you become more engrossed in your loved one's life than in your own, you can quickly experience the sense of losing yourself in an unbalanced relationship. Know how to play the best leading role in your own movie, before signing on as costar to another. The key to harmonic balance is to stay focused on enjoying the journey, while recognizing and respecting the individual path of another.

Sound selfish? Good! If everyone was more selfish about loving themselves first, hate could not exist; nor war, nor crime, nor any sense of separation. Engaging with other people only after you have taken the time to align with positive thoughts and good feeling energy is always the path of least resistance. Not to mention you also get to be the positive example for your loved ones to listen to their higher self, and stay true to their own intentions.

I know this can make perfect sense when we look at the examples of other people's lives. I also know what a struggle it can be to apply what we know to every area of our own life and relationships. It is easy to believe that when we love someone, they hold the magic wand to make us happy, or sad, in the blink of an eye. It certainly feels that way more times than not. Some of us also want to believe that we have the same superhuman strength to save, fix, rescue, control, or change another—in the name of love. After all, it would be easier if everyone else would just do what pleases us most. Or so we think.

I too have lived in this land of wishes and make believe for most of my life. Desperately wanting to believe the depth of my love for another is the exception to any universal rule and beyond. However, as the capable and competent free will spirits we all are, not one single person has the power or authority to force anyone else to think, feel, or act in a certain way. We may choose to adapt and conform, to appease a more dominating personality than ours, but the soul always knows the truth and freedom of love.

Let's take a birds-eye view of the game of love. We see many people out on the playing field who haven't got a clue what the rules are—or even how to play the game, because pretty much everything we have been told about love is a lie. I know that's a bold statement but nevertheless, it is still true. We can see it in the unhappy, unhealthy, damaged, and dysfunctional players running blindly all around us.

Traditionally, the most common template for romantic coupling fosters more of an intertwining of lives, and ongoing co-dependency. Rather than encouraging individual identity and personal fulfillment, we attempt to merge two brains into one mind. In fact, the very free spirited energy which ignites the spark to begin with, is often stifled or destroyed when confined by a box of conforming rules. Instead of relating with each other in new and exciting ways, we typically gravitate back to familiar territory.

Many of us were raised with fallacies and fairytales. Starry eyed dreamers in pursuit of our one true love, anxiously awaiting the amazing someone to fill the role of best friend and romantic lover—to have and to hold into the sunset and beyond. A Cloud Nine union of two souls uniting as one, with the joyous expectation of living happily ever after. Deep down, there are a great number of people who still want to believe in these dreamy visions of perfection, especially if they have witnessed far more of the opposite.

Speaking of which, I would love to dispel some archaic ideologies still in existence about romantic love. One of the biggest myths out there, which can offer a tremendous amount of heartache, is the belief that you could be born requiring another half to make you whole. There is still an overwhelming majority who insist we all have that perfect match, the one who holds the key to our hearts and pieces to our puzzle.

We hear many refer to this individual as a soulmate or the even more elusive twin flame. It then becomes our mission, and sometimes life-long task, to find the yin to our yang, and the true love of our life who completes us. That's what the best love stories and hopeless romantics are telling us, anyway.

The universal truth is, everyone who is currently here with us on the same planet and in our time/space reality, are different version of "soul mates." In fact anyone who sparks a strong reaction within you, aka "lights your fire," is an amazing representation of who and what you are connecting with at a soul/spiritual level. They teach you how to comfort and nurture yourself back to love. Other mates can validate your inner beauty, inspiring and encouraging your authentic self the freedom to shine.

According to Law of Attraction, you are the original vibrating signal for all that comes your way. This also means you are playing on the same level as anyone in your reality—especially those who occupy your full attention. Therefore, no one else can really insert themselves into your life without your permission. Regardless of who is in front of you, or what is happening around you, you are always the one who is creating, inviting and participating in your own experience.

The entire focus of the previous chapters can be summarized here again: what you believe, you will receive; what you expect, you will get. If you live by default, sleepwalking through life with an attitude of waiting, missing, and feeling incomplete, you will attract more people and experiences to confirm your current beliefs. When you choose a deliberate practice of focusing on thoughts that feel good to you, you can then attract companions who operate from the same positive mindset.

Without a doubt, there exists a powerful essence of divine oneness in the human experience. Naturally inspiring the desire to unite our life, love, and laughter with other like-minded playmates. There are obvious reasons why the human species has pretty much followed the same method of dating and mating since the beginning of time.

Some are brought together through familial, cultural, or religious beliefs, others for convenience, security, and financial gain. Most often we are drawn together through physical, mental and/or spiritual attraction.

Unfortunately, we see some people rush to the altar, only to be disillusioned when the honeymoon is over. Many people marry with the hope that their spouse will never change, and many more with the hope that they will. It really comes down to personal desire, this relationship to a companion at a particular time in our constantly changing lives. Historically, we tend to follow the example of our parents, friends, society, and cultures—or we are determined to create the opposite.

What most of us fail to realize is that who we are in our youth, as we excitedly say "I Do" to one person for eternity, is going to change and transform over the years and decades naturally. Perhaps we were taught to believe that commitment means you have a legally binding agreement of for better or worse, in sickness and in health, until death parts us, in promising to never change our minds, and make that work forever.

Can you see why this measure of success is so difficult to live up to? Let's be clear, choosing to stay in a loveless marriage, because you think you signed a life-long contract, is not a commitment to love. The commitment to love is simply recognizing when you have outgrown your best reasons for being together, and treating each other with kindness and respect throughout the transition.

It's not that couples who are together for 50 or more years have the magical secret to lasting love and happy relationships. It means that they found a way to stay together that works for both of them, or at least they are not killing each other in the process. The truth is everyone is not meant to have lifelong togetherness with only one person. Nor is this a necessary requirement in order to fully understand meaningful partnerships and the commitment to authentic love.

In actuality, love has no need for a book of rules in order to exist. There are no ceremonies, rituals, or contracts that will ever be needed to solidify a loving connection with another. No matter how strong your beliefs and intentions are, or your beloved's, there are no vows, exchanging of rings, or changing of names that will ensure the same mutual devotion until the end of time. It is a beautiful ideal, but if love really worked this way, there would be no divorce, no extramarital affairs, and no living out the rest of your days with someone you grow more to dislike than desire.

No matter who you are with, or for how long, the number one thing you can do to ruin any relationship is to be ruled by your issues and insecurities. If you do not allow yourselves the freedom to have time and space to continue developing as individuals, you will create an unhealthy dependency. Even, and especially, most long-lasting companionships need room to breathe and opportunities to miss each other. This is when absence truly does make the heart grow fonder, and creates the reminders of what we love and appreciate.

Until each person can take ownership of their own thoughts, emotions, and behaviors, the possibility for harmony in any relationship will remain an ongoing struggle. Unfortunately, most will decide they chose the wrong partner instead of looking at themselves, often seeking a new flame, as a crutch or distraction, before ending the current partnership. Without question, this route will always be a temporary fix to a permanent solution—we must learn to love ourselves first.

Digging through the Dirty Laundry

It is incredibly apparent, as we listen to countless stories of devastation and destruction, just how many people have a hard time being faithful to one person for life. Even though many have attempted the dangerous high-wire act of juggling two worlds at once, someone inevitably gets hurt. Anytime you overlap your intimate relationships, pursuing a new attraction while still saying "I love you" to someone else, you are playing with fire. Few will escape without getting burned and the casualties can be devastating.

I know I may ruffle some feathers here, but infidelity is not just about the act of having a secret sexual or emotional companion outside of a marriage or mutual agreement of monogamy. Frankly, no other person can insert themselves into a relationship that is solid and happy to begin with. In most cases, the growing disconnection and mounting issues between the couple were happening long before the thoughts about "cheating" ever began.

Sadly, instead of courageously facing the uncomfortable choice of fixing the cracks in their current relationship, or ending the partnership and all that they built together, people often will seek satisfaction by the easiest avenues possible. Even the most loyal and true can be tempted by a secret escape, typically opting for a stimulating outlet which will offer the least disruption to their current life, and a way to feel excited again.

We are obviously in a world with many other people who may, or may not, get our attention. It is human nature to notice our attraction to another body, mind, or soul. However, when we are deeply and positively connected to the person with whom we share our life, love and dreams with, nothing and no one else will quite compare. Nor can anyone really come between two people who thoroughly enjoy being with each other more than anyone else. People who are completely satisfied in their relationships, have no desire to risk what they have for anyone different. Before searching for greener grass, know that you did everything possible to take care of your own lawn first.

What this really breaks down to is the moral compass of each individual's character. If you are someone who expects honesty and respect from others, then you must live it, in order to have it. When you engage in something you have to hide from the ones you love, you are not in positive alignment with your truth or theirs. Regardless of the depth of deceit, the truth is always under the surface, and the truth will always set you free.

There are many who will seek comfort and companionship in a new partner, before truly resolving the unfinished business in the current relationship. The same pattern will most likely continue until there is a personal commitment to satisfaction and security within. Do yourself, and every future relationship, a favor: get really clear about who you are and what you want now. Then find the kindest and gentlest way to express your clarity, with whoever it may concern, and allow the chips to fall where they may.

Realistically, very few will jump at the chance to initiate a conversation that we believe will not be well received. If you are like the majority of people, you refrain from being completely honest about your relationship because you do not want to hurt your loved one's feelings, or worse. Candidly, it does feel like an easier option to just hide some of our truth rather than deal with any unwanted consequences. Inevitably, this route actually does more harm than good for all parties. When you protect someone from their own feelings, you are only delaying their ability to make their own choices and know their own strength, not to mention, you are also making a deeper statement that you are uncomfortable with your own emotions in this light. Regardless of the words said or suppressed, you always know the truth.

Sadly, most couples delay the critical check-ins with each other, until there is so much wrong between them that it seems too much to make right. I'm not talking about the superficial disagreements and power struggles which normally lead nowhere. I am referring to those real and raw heart-to-hearts that put all of your cards on the table. When you set the stage to communicate your truth with your partner, especially about your relationship, you will avoid wasting time consoling hurt feelings, or getting lost in head games with more questions than answers.

So let's get down to the nitty gritty and undress the layers and illusions about sex, love, and intimacy. Very simply, sex and love do not necessarily go hand in hand, but when combined, have the potential for infinite levels of euphoria. You can be intimate without having physical contact, and you can also have sexual intercourse and never make love. When you are feeling love and appreciation for the person you are intimately sharing your mind, body, and soul with… you are in the magical energy of making love.

Ironically, most people are uncomfortable even discussing the subject of sex, and yet every creature on this planet is born with the natural drive and basic instinct. Obviously we know humans unite in sexual pleasure for more reasons than just to have children. In fact, I'm sure if the physical sensation of orgasm was not as incredible as it is, there would be far fewer people doing it, and therefore, a much smaller human population. The chaos around this topic is formed when we are expected to believe our sexuality is something wrong, naughty, dirty, bad, a sin, or shameful part of us that should be hidden.

If sex is treated as anything but a kind and mutual expression of attraction, there is such mass confusion, damage to relationships, sexual disease transmission, and even horrific abuse. When two people are physically attracted to each other, the topic of sex will inevitably need to be addressed. Have mature and responsible conversations upfront and then stick to it or agree to something else. In this way you can immediately find clear and appropriate common ground, on what can be a huge make-or-break issue in relationships and potentially a life-altering decision.

Cleaning out the Closet

An overwhelming number of people are shouting out for authentic intimacy, and yet they are working extremely hard to protect themselves from it. When we first meet, it is natural to try to present the best version of ourselves to impress another. Just as we do when we interview for any job we want, shining the spotlight on our best features and minimizing anything that may seem to be undesirable. As time goes on, and more of the inside truth is revealed, the real test of compatibility begins.

Awareness of loving emotions within, especially when we focus on another, is an exhilarating discovery. When the object of our affection is offering a matching vibration, both can experience the "falling in love" stage of connection, the incredible sensation that takes our breath away and makes our hearts skip a beat.

From a bigger perspective, what is actually happening? Like-minded energies completely aligned with the loving source of their own beautiful light, recognized and reflected in the eyes and expressions of the other. Both are being stimulated, through their mutual attraction and adoration, to the next greatest version of self. When we are in the early stages of such blissful intoxication, it is enticing to believe the same giddy intensity will carry us to our "happily ever after." Those who have experienced this hypnotic fire can easily resonate with the magnetic attraction of meeting a divine match. The male or female version of ourselves who gets our attention in such a magical way inspires us to evolve to our highest and best, both in their presence and beyond.

Even the wisest and most self-aware among us can be swept away by the thrill of getting lost in love with another. The key is to continue holding the friendship in a loving and sacred space, no matter what—agreeing to ground rules and boundaries, early in the relationship in order to openly and honestly acknowledge any obstacles to positive development as they occur.

For some, they will move forward with their best friend and most intimate partner, excitedly taking on the world together. For others, the storm clouds of doubt and insecurity may creep in to rain on their parade, sadly, due to an increasing need to protect ourselves from getting burned by the very flame we were initially enticed by. This in itself is a very natural and human response when we realize we may have deep emotions and strong affection for another person, or they for us.

However, the "turn on" can easily switch to terror, if we are not genuinely ready for what may come next. There may be numerous reasons, on the surface, why someone will pull away from the very thing they were initially drawn to. The bottom line will always be when the fear of moving too far outside their current comfort zone becomes stronger than the desire for the relationship to progress or even continue. The best way to navigate through any contradiction or change of heart, is through clarifying communication with kindness. And the sooner, the better.

Unfortunately, many adults lack the courageous maturity to initiate this type of dialog. Instead, they will do everything in their power to steer clear of the truth. Spending precious time and wasted energy in avoidance of possible confrontation, unwanted emotions and any conversations. Choosing to either silently slip away, or pacify the other party just enough. Sadly, both directions lead nowhere, leaving the lost and bewildered person searching for a way and a reason that makes sense to them.

Often what happens when we are not completely ready to be authentically seen and heard, we will habitually repeat old patterns with new partners until we are ready for authenticity. Many people have foolishly found themselves, at one time or too many to count, participating in the oldest and most common dance of dysfunction in civilization: known as the dynamic duo of the "Runner" and the "Chaser." It is a mind game of assumptions, second guessing, and emotional unavailability in a losing battle of wit and wills. Sound fun?

Here's how it works. The Runner, usually the more masculine energy of the two, experiences fear about the relationship and silently retreats to safety. The Chaser, typically the feminine energy, fears loss of connection and desperately pursues it. If the hero returns to save the day, the waiting wounded feels loved and wanted again, thus triggering the next chase. The previously abandoned one clings even tighter, and the smothered one struggles for more space to breathe. This cycle is unhealthy and painful but it will never really end until the runner stops running, or the chaser gives up the chase. The roles can reverse, as well as the partners, but both dancers are always being drawn to the same dance, they are reacting to the same underlying fear of exposing hidden flaws and insecurities to be potentially judged, ridiculed, or rejected, inevitably blocking the exact experience they both joined together for.

A true reality of genuine connection, regardless of romantic involvement, will require a deeper level of visibility and a willingness to be seen. When we attempt to read our loved ones' minds, or expect them to read ours, we set ourselves up for major disappointment and misunderstandings. It is much easier to learn how to listen as well as how to clearly and appropriately state your perspective. Many times people have already been telling us their truth, but we can hear only what we want to hear.

Whenever we delay an unwanted conversation, especially for the sake of protecting feelings, we only make things harder. The truth may hurt temporarily, but never as much as the permanent confusion from everything left unsaid. Even though it is not always apparent why something so sweet can suddenly turn sour, how many broken hearts are left with more questions than answers in the dust of devastation?

Save yourself a lot of time, tears, and tantrums, for a few minutes of being vulnerably uncomfortable. Instead of sweeping issues under the rug and repeatedly blowing things off, be the one to initiate the thoughtful discussions anytime there is a need for clarity and resolution between you. Respectfully express your own fears, concerns, or any change of heart about the relationship as soon as the appropriate time arises. Thank your partner for sharing in your life, regardless of how long it has been or what has happened up to this point. This conduct is actually what makes you personally stronger and a better future companion to others.

Plain and simply, we are drawn to the people who best represent any of our own unfinished business and/or soul work that needs enlightenment. We will continue to attract, and be attracted to, exactly who we truly believe we need and deserve. The more time we spend on feeding our own mind, body and spirit with the satisfying resource of love, the better prepared we are to cross paths with an amazing and joyful matching energy. Allow the continual possibility for the companionship you seek, instead of waiting for a specific meeting to recreate the connection for you. Perfect partners can come in all sizes and flavors, and at different phases of our journey—most can probably be deemed an appropriate match in a given period of time. There exists the possibility of incredible connections that are best served in days, months, years, or for several decades. We see many shades of gray in our own lives as well as the expanding window to the world. No matter what version of a mate we want to experience, as we develop our personality and preferences along the way, everyone ultimately wants the same thing—the freedom to be who we really are, loved and accepted no matter what.

If you continue to participate in unproductive patterns in your relationships, the players may come and go, but the game never ends. History will continue to repeat itself until you become aware of your own limiting beliefs and behaviors. You will never prevent the past from tainting your future by living a life of lies and recycled dysfunction. However, you can have a fresh start through hindsight and the wisdom of awareness.

You will no longer participate in the insanity of doing the same thing over and over, expecting different results.

Just as we need a mirror to see how we look, everyone in our reality is a reflection of what's already happening on the inside of us. The people around us are showing us how we feel about what we are observing. It often feels like other people are the reason we feel a certain way, but that's impossible. When we notice those characteristics and behaviors in others that we like, or don't like, we are actually observing parts of ourselves in action. The sooner we pay attention to the beautiful similarities between us, the better we will understand and love the differences.

Blame, or even credit, for the so-called success or failure of any relationship is pointless. Simply recognize each experience as an opportunity for greater self-awareness, a catalyst to help you continually expand and be a better person. Let go of the ego's need to be right and follow the soul's right to be happy. The quicker you can acknowledge and embrace your own imperfections, the easier it will be to release expectations that other people need to be flawless in order for your world to be perfect. Every soul is here to learn how to coexist with each other. We teach people how to treat us by how we treat ourselves. The absolute best rule of thumb, anytime we have upsetting thoughts and emotions about another, is to take the necessary time out and focus on our own positive alignment first. Equally important is the realization that not everyone we encounter is meant to be a part of our daily lives forever. The purpose for most meetings is to refine the ongoing clarity of what we prefer now, as a result of our insights, acquired throughout the relationship.

Let's be honest, we see far too many examples in society, and possibly in our own families, of the blindly determined and stubbornly confused. Those insisting they can win the same war of insanity, in spite of those who fought and failed for centuries before them. Clinging to relationships which no longer have a viable pulse, the only thing really holding them together is their refusal to call time of death and allow transition to a better place. Why do they stay even though it's obvious their togetherness is no longer offering a positive and loving connection? For the most part, they have settled in the belief that any other option will bring even worse dissatisfaction and more disappointment than what is currently being endured. The adamantly resistant will insist that if their beloved would just change this or that, then everything else would be fine. However, the longer we stay in the mindset that our partner has to correct something in order for us to be comfortable, the longer we stay stuck spinning on that broken record forever.

Regardless of the present issue(s) between us, length of time together and any promises made, kept or broken—if nothing changes, nothing changes. We will never really get to the source of discord, by continuing to focus on surface "problems." Typically, there are many things that rise to the top, as time goes by, but there will always be an underlying common theme to be addressed and positively directed. Until then, each will stand firm in their convictions, pointing at the other as the reason for their discontent, ignoring the white flag of surrender.

The real reason these unions are so much more difficult than others, is because they are built on shaky ground to begin with: an unhealthy mixture of predominantly more negative/fear-based energy than positive/love-based energy. Both individuals, with unhealed wounds and unmet needs, are searching for someone to make it better, and this exchange can go on for as long as both are chained to protecting their own injuries. Unfortunately there are still far too many unions generating so much poison, that the toxicity will be felt by generations to come. Let me be extremely clear about this, anytime there is physical, emotional, or mental abuse, there is an enormous amount of unresolved fear, hurt, and anger brewing inside both the "abuser" and the "abused." As a child who grew up in such an environment, I can honestly say that domestic violence is never about one person's problem and the helpless victims who love them. It takes two to tango, but it will take only one to end the dance of doom.

Truth of character is often seen most clearly when someone feels they are threatened or backed into a corner in some way. When someone is mad, sad, or afraid...these are the times when any hidden demons can come out to play. Believing that someone is one person with you and a different person with everyone else is extremely naïve. If you believe you are the exception it is only because you haven't been the target—yet. It's easy to be nice and affectionate when all is well in our world. However, who we are when the chips are down is when our true colors are seen.

The bottom line is that people do not inflict suffering unless they suffer within. There can be no mistreatment of other people, or animals for that matter, unless the individual is operating from a much darker place of personal trauma and tragedy. Nor, do people allow themselves to be a victim of abuse, unless they are already operating from low self-esteem in a powerless mentality. Despite the excuses and cries of denial, choosing to stay in pain-inflicted partnerships is not because of an undying, saintly love for our loved ones. It is actually a constant craving to satisfy a deeper hunger, to believe we are worthy and deserving of love. Without question, if there is abuse or addiction in any form, there is an underlying fear of inadequacy and lack of complete self-appreciation in both parties.

The perception for most people is that if you leave the abuser, alcoholic, or addict, you leave the problem behind you. In dangerous cases, the best solution indeed is immediate protection and safety. Professional guidance and positive direction for all parties affected is also extremely critical. You can leave a house and geographical location but every family member will take their scars and confused minds with them, especially when minor children are watching and following in your footsteps. If you believe they are too young to understand what's happening in their home, you are sadly mistaken. The young and impressionable are actually far more aware and accepting of the truth than adults are. The objective is to be the healthiest and most responsible parent you can be, so your kids can enjoy being kids.

If you truly want to fix your relationships and end generational cycles of abuse, the obvious and healthiest route is to take the necessary time to take care of yourself first, allowing each party the space to take ownership of their own flaws and the individual responsibility to get better. When you know how to love yourself through any darkness, you will never be trapped in it again.

What to Keep, What to Give Away and What to Burn

When you keep your focus on following your own bliss, as well as developing from your natural abilities and inner beauty, you will never need another person to do this for you. Of course, it always feels good when you are recognized with a compliment, especially from someone you love, pointing out the things about you that are admired and appreciated. However, their words and actions will never be enough to permanently replace anything you believe is missing to begin with. From your foundation of self-love, you will have the strongest basis to love another without the pain of conditions.

We always need to remember that we are never done evolving and expanding. The expectation of timeless perfection, especially when combining our life with another, is one of the greatest illusions of mankind. Our relationships will inevitably move through many changes, just as each individual does. Allowing the natural course to play out is the real secret to success in any companionship. Remaining true to ourselves is the most important component of open and honest communication with our significant someone.

Believe it or not, it is quite possible to never again be a victim of the dreaded "heartbreak" experience; it is still plaguing the walking wounded and has since the beginning of time. There is the overwhelming sense of being swept off our feet, only to be left alone to pick up the shattered pieces off the floor. No matter the reasons for ending, or length of time together, we can endure a great deal of suffering when we believe we have been cut off from a deep and meaningful connection. Something that once offered tremendous pleasure, can suddenly feel like we have been pushed into an unwanted reality of hurt, anger, sadness, confusion, and gut-wrenching grief. In an attempt to rationalize our way out of the pain, we will analyze every detail in recycled thoughts of "whys" and "what ifs," replaying sad songs and painful memories as we mourn for a love, we believe, that we no longer have access to.

We become consumed with questioning the validity of the entire relationship, as well as our own inadequacies. We feel humiliated by the belief that we were being foolishly vulnerable, we offered our heart on a silver platter to the "wrong" person. As a result, we are left second-guessing our ability to make good choices, now and in the future— always, in the back of our mind, hoping for a return of the love we are continually missing.

Typically people who take repeated trips to Heartbreak Hotel, are the same ones who seem to struggle with maintaining a positive mindset and emotional well-being for any length of time. The actual devastation, which can be fueled to become a torturous obsession, is the false belief that a specific person, and/or circumstance, is the one and only cure to make us feel better again. Believing the source of love and happiness can be given and taken away by other people will always be the real heartache associated with love. I understand how hard this may be to swallow, especially when we are in the depth of our pain. Nonetheless, it is important to understand that love and hurt are never synonymous. There is only positive alignment in the energy of love, or the resistance of that energy. Any experience of painful emotions is directly related to the conditions and expectations that are made in the name of love.

There is always more to the story than the words we speak and the image we present to the outside world. Who we really are is the person hidden behind closed doors. We can see the obvious truth in people with whom we really have no emotional attachment. However, with the people we love most, we will pretend, ignore, and make excuses—turning a blind eye time and time again. The depth of our misery really has nothing to do with how much we love the other person. In fact, any discomfort we may experience in life is always because we are resisting an unwanted reality, the awful gap between what we see as our current unwanted circumstance, and what we desire to be true. Negative emotions only occur to let us know when our thoughts are not in alignment with the positive flow of love, the source of who we really are.

If we take time out from our sadness long enough to observe, we can easily go to all different places in our mind in a matter of minutes or even seconds, whether someone is actually in front of us, conversing and responding, or not. We can play out any past and future interactions with our own thoughts with such great intensity, that we can feel the sensation as if it is actually happening right now.

We can relive memories, envision the future, and have a present emotional response to all of it, solely generated from our current perspective, imagination, and desire. If this is true, and I have not seen or heard any evidence to the contrary, then we always have a choice about our thoughts and feelings, in relationship to any other, as well as all circumstances we are faced with.

Since I know this can be such a painfully intense experience, I want to offer some additional guidance to assist in walking through the sorrow of separation, for until we can really find acceptance in the present, as well as eliminate our belief that something is missing, we will continue to limit ourselves from the full benefit of ourselves. The direction of comfort and relief will always flow through the natural path of least resistance—love.

So what do you do when the ache inside is so overwhelming that you wonder if you will ever truly be happy for the rest of your life? When the missing runs so deep that you question if you will ever feel completely connected to love again, or even if you want to. When no matter how much time goes by, your mind still longs for a different reality. You may even believe your anguish is much bigger than anyone can comprehend, or possibly recover from.

There are many of us who have walked this path and, as difficult as it was, have discovered the road to a new joy in a meaningful life. Practicing your own healthy and beneficial ways to release any agony going on inside, will always offer more opportunities for relief. Laugh when you want to laugh, cry when you want to cry, scream out at the sky, or punch something made for punching. Choose whatever natural and healthy options that will offer mental, physical, and emotional comfort. Share with those who can offer an empathetic ear and a safe place to land, as well as encouraging movement forward.

Most importantly, treat yourself as your own best friend—with an enormous amount of kindness, understanding, and empowering support, just as you would for someone you love.

Allow your own process of healing, day by day, at the pace that feels best for you. As much as well-intentioned friends try, no one can push you into acceptance, including you. Spend as much quality time alone as possible and less time in negative distraction and influence from others. Again, be completely selfish and find, or create, the safest sanctuary to retreat and transform into the next greatest version of yourself.

The goal is to fill up any internal emptiness, with the connective flow of love and positive energy available to you right here and now. Commit to self-care and feeling better as your top priority, a daily and deliberate effort of redirecting your thoughts, words and actions to those which bring you the most relief and comfort. As time goes on, you will get extremely deliberate and particular about the energy you fuel your body with. Quickly noticing when negative energy is starting to get the best of you, you can immediately turn your attention to better feeling thoughts. This steady practice will gradually allow the crippling waves of emotion to subside to a gentle sway, safely cradled in the arms of love and peace.

Life offers a buffet of experiences to love, learn, and grow from. We naturally get very attached to people, things, and we fall in love with a variety of scenarios along the way. However, to keep yourself from falling into a pit of despair, always remember there is a much bigger picture in motion than what most can observe from behind their own eyes and injuries. Each soul is on a journey of evolvement in their own timeframe. No other's desire, no matter how strong, can ever change the course of a free willed spirit in flight.

The good news is that no other person on this planet, or series of events, will ever need to change in order for you to be happy. You get to be happy right this second, if that's what you decide. The only thing necessary is that you accept your current reality to be exactly what you created and needed up to this point. It is the perfect opportunity for healing, growth and appreciation. You can change your reality at any time you become dissatisfied, simply by changing your mind about the true source and solution of your happiness—which is always you. Continually remind yourself that no matter who you love or miss in the human experience, you are always an individual soul who is in this dimension for your own spiritual desires. This physical arena offers endless avenues to fulfill your passion and purpose with other people and experiences to treasure. Just like the magical rainbow which appears after the darkest storm, you can use your nightmares as the inspiring motivation to achieve your dreams. There will, once again, be a reason for the sun to shine, laughter to relieve your loss and a genuine smile in the place of heartache.

The healthiest avenue, through anything undesirable, is to keep focusing your attention on being the happiest you can be right now. The sooner you can allow the process of healing, and adapt to your new normal, the sooner you will get to experience a frequency of love with no sense of time and space— neither a true beginning or end. We are all in the same process of experimenting our way to awareness, transforming through the energy of love, over and over again.

Choosing to channel positive energy for yourself, and holding all others in the highest light when we think of them, may sound like we are sticking our head in the sand or in denial about our reality. In fact, nothing could be further from the truth. We are actually wide awake and openly aware when we are always searching for the best feeling thoughts on any subject, not only respecting ourselves, but the people we love as well. Learning to calmly manage ourselves, and understand the perspective of our partners along the way, will bring far better times than bad times. Instead of repeating the drama and trauma of good love gone bad, I propose you fall in love with your own life—right where you are. No matter your current circumstance, you already know if you are truly satisfied in all avenues of your life or not. The best thing you can do for you, not to mention any current relationship, is to stop everything you have been doing that has not worked so far. Instead, commit to keeping the focus on your ability to change your own mind and get happy no matter what.

Before setting yourself up to fall again, please allow the necessary time to regroup and know yourself in a more confident light. Treat yourself as the one you enjoy being with the most. Fill your mind with thoughts that nurture and empower you. Replace behaviors that no longer serve you, with those that are more in line with the highest version of you. Surround yourself with influential positive energy to bring comfort, calm and wellbeing to you. You are beginning to create the most amazing masterpiece of you, from a blank canvas of wonderment.

Chapter 6: Get Well Soon

Prepare yourself, as this will definitely be the most brutally honest chapter, not to mention when tough love will apply the most. Not because I believe in scare tactics, but due to the proof of my own life and demise of my loved ones, I have witnessed firsthand the severity of natural consequences when you live your life under the illusion that you are not the one in charge of your own health and well-being.

Even though I am giving you a serious message in this chapter, I truly believe laughter is always the best medicine and healthiest outlet to manage any source of pain. Some of my favorite memories have come from the final weeks of my cousin's stay in hospice. Just imagine a Jerry Springer show filmed live at the deathbed and you pretty much have the idea of what went down. Fortunately, I completely understand how the best and the worst in people will come out in a time of intense emotions and grief. I also know it's perfectly okay to laugh through the tears, and in fact, laughter is often what keeps us sane through the insanity.

I dedicate my entire book, but especially this chapter, to my double cousin and one of my best friends, Kelli. She was born Kelli Rae Clendenen. She was given the devastating diagnosis of glioblastoma brain cancer, stage four, because there is no cure and a maximum of five more years to live on the day of her 46th birthday. This marked the beginning of the end for a wounded warrior, already in a battle with life.

The proceeding chain of events still leaves many of my family members in shock, but I cannot deny that it does make sense according to universal truth. Kelli's dad, my uncle Ray, was also diagnosed with brain cancer just a few weeks after his daughter. He died within two months. Several years prior, Kelli's sister Michelle died in her 30s of a drug overdose. My uncle was determined to leave the planet before enduring the horrific grief of burying another of his children, and he did.

Sadly for the rest of us, after 15 months of multiple brain surgeries and other quality of life treatments to ease the pain, in attempts to extend her life, Kelli released her failing body on June 13, 2016. My conversations with Kelli in those final months, weeks, days, and hours will stay with me forever. True to my promise, I am sharing her experience from a much different perspective about the mind, body, and soul connection—in life, health, love, and the after-life.

It is difficult for me to summarize such a kind and courageous soul in just a few words or paragraphs, but for the sake of this message, I will do my best: Kelli was light, love, beauty, laughter, fun, humility, honesty, open, understanding, hard-working, nurturing, caring, comforting, friendly, compassionate, thoughtful, intensely emotional, sensitive, empathic, investigative, determined, protective, loyal, genuine, spirited, stubborn, vocal, fearful and self-critical.

What many people didn't know is that Kelli had the same curse, aka gift, as me and so many of our tortured family members. She was extremely empathic and intuitive, could actually see the color of a soul's aura and was especially connected to animals. The people who knew her best also know she deprived herself of her own love, acceptance, and full appreciation of her naturally powerful light.

In our conversations leading up to my cousin's death, Kelli was the first to admit that she didn't make her life, health, or self, a priority. Even with the stakes so high, she was willing to put her body through extreme lifesaving measures, but she just couldn't break away from the poisonous energy fueling her mind. I could see the quicksand of negative emotion that was making her sicker, and I also knew the thoughts behind it. I have no doubt that this is the true source of any disease, as well as the accelerating fuel of decline.

More than anything in life, Kelli wanted to be a mom. Her wish was granted twice and she spent the rest of her life making her children the center of her world. Growing up with the same chaotic family dynamic, I completely understood the desire to experience a different world of love through our children's eyes.

However, just as I have seen generations of history repeat themselves in my son's addiction, we can never change our own past by attempting to recreate the opposite for, or through, our children. Our offspring are not here to clean up our unfinished business, or fulfill our own dreams and aspirations, but they can show us a better way forward if we allow them to be who they are, free spirits having their own human experience.

Despite the enormous amount of family and friends who easily fell in love with Kelli, she would continually return to the torturous belief that she wasn't loved as deeply as she loved others. The middle child of five strong willed children, she professed the need to be the loudest, or the reason for concern, just to be noticed. From a young age, Kelli had a wide range of mishaps and accidents which would offer a temporary spot light, regardless of whether the attention was positive or negative—she craved it.

As an adult, my cousin spent a great deal of time in mental anguish and emotional upset over past events, fear of the unknown, and anything in the present that felt out of her control. We spent countless hours on the phone as I naturally volunteered to become her wellness coach and, selfishly, I didn't want to lose her. However, even from Kelli's death bed, barely able to speak, she was worried if the insurance was going to pay for hospice. I knew then that she would never truly know freedom until she left the human experience.

Especially in her final months, Kelli hated being alone with her own thoughts and emotions. She constantly wanted to be surrounded by people she loved. She thrived on bringing humor and the raw truth to any discussion. If my cousin wasn't making people laugh, she was sharing in their tears, but the impact of her spirit was felt by all. In private, she was extremely hard on herself as she judged her character defects and any believed physical imperfections critically. All of this ultimately, and negatively, affected the health of her mind and body.

Much as I have learned to embrace my ability to see what each soul is most likely creating for themselves, it is never easy to witness the unhealthy and self-sabotaging lifestyles of my loved ones. I also knew I was being shown a mirror of my own critical thinking still preventing my own happiness. Not only was I going to be coaching my cousin to freedom, I was going to do it for myself. Even before her diagnosis of a terminal illness, I was aware that Kelli's repeated bouts of sickness and harmful accidents, were all signs of deeper trouble brewing inside. I was determined to do everything in my power to slow down the fast-moving train on its way to derailment. Unfortunately, I had already learned the hard way, we cannot love someone enough to show them their wake up calls, change their mind, or prevent their path. Many of the people I grew up loving could easily have been labeled as the craziest, unhealthiest, meanest, most damaged, and self-tortured members of society. Regardless of the degree of dysfunction or diagnosis, there was an underlying loyalty to blood that became a love I would unquestionably sacrifice my own life for. In fact, this was the only kind of love I knew for a very long time. I refused myself any peace or happiness if anyone I cared about was suffering, which sadly, was too many to count.

I can now understand, without a shadow of a doubt, why I purposely chose to join this particular group of souls known as my family. You have probably heard of us as one of those sad families out there who are labeled cursed, suffering tragedy after tragedy with little time to process or grieve in between. If you are someone like me, a bleeding heart attempting to heal the world, you will struggle dreadfully in the concern for the people you love most. All I knew was a desire to save people from their own demise, but I was rapidly destroying myself in the process.

Before I was 13, my paternal grandfather committed suicide, so I was pretty much prepped for death and devastation from the start. I watched my dad deal with his grief by drinking himself deeper into the bottle, and I watched everyone else grasp for their own ways to cope and make sense out of the madness. I don't remember all of the details of the suicide, but I am fully aware of the toxic beliefs that will cause someone to take their own life, as well as the devastation and destruction that it leaves behind. What I realize most is, no matter what, we ultimately create our own demise.

In story after story, there is always a universal factor at play—you will die as you lived. If you have no appreciation for your health, or for your life, you will probably not live very long. The sooner you go with the flow, the smoother you gently float down the stream to an ocean of eternal happiness. I'm pretty sure everyone is aware of what constitutes an unhealthy habit by now, but let's revisit it anyway, as a refresher on common sense. You will not have long-lasting health if you remain committed to digesting and inhaling toxins and chemicals, eating mostly processed foods and little or no exercise. Treating alcohol, drugs, pills, and smoking, as part of your nutritive food groups, is not on any wellness chart.

On top of that, the Law of Attraction is matching your vibration. If you live your life in negative energy, continually feeding off chaos, drama, and stress, you will spend most of your days in a great deal of mental and/or physical discomfort. If you are an adrenaline junky, always living on the edge, you will most likely die in the act of seeking the next thrill, but it will typically be called a fluke or an "accident." Even the heroes of society, like policemen or firefighters, those who give their lives for the betterment of humanity, already know the dangers and risks involved. When you have a higher calling, you have the courage to die for it.

I have heard it stated that everyone eventually kills themselves and, from everything I have observed, I believe this to be true. The bottom line is, when you have had enough of this world, you will return to the source of perfect love, eternally evolving to whatever adventure your soul wants to experience next. As with any other possessions in this lifetime, the better you take care of yourself, the longer you will last. I believe we all have ample warning, and ultimately the final say, as to when and how we will leave the human experience. My mission is to let people know how to be free, while they are still alive.

Here's the real deal, regardless of the time we take our first breath, or the last, our life is what we believe to be true in every second in between. We are born with an open ended return date, in this temporary human experience, on purpose. The daily choices we make for our mind and body, will inevitably determine when and how our trip will end.

Sadly, most people do not pay attention to their emotional wellbeing as the necessary ingredient to perfect health. Also, ignoring the multiple signs and variety of wake up calls designed to get our attention, when we are off track. Lacking the awareness of personal power, we believe we can become helpless victims to illness, disease, genetics, and statistics. In fact, those conditions are the result of not treating yourself well to begin with. The majority of people will put off making changes until the stakes are so high, they feel they have no choice but to give up or fight.

Which is exactly where my beautiful cousin found herself—with a life-threatening illness that she had feared for her entire life, and at the same time unknowingly created. Am I suggesting that Kelli deserved to get brain cancer and die at 47? Certainly not, nor does anyone deserve that fate. However, the undeniable universal truth is what you continue to feed is what will grow.

I saw the living proof of someone's lifelong expectation, and worst fear, come true. From the time my cousin was really little, any harmless change or new spot on her body, in her mind, was imagined as the next cancer scare. Top that with years of feeling unloved and unworthy and you have the perfect breeding ground for sickness and serious injuries to occur.

In our final conscious conversation, I asked Kelli if this is how she saw that her death would play out when she was little, and she instantly said, "Yes, exactly like this." I knew then, if I couldn't save her life, I was committed to do everything in my power to make her transition as beautiful and free of pain as possible. After a relatively short amount of time on earth, seeking much of her acceptance and approval from the outside world, my cousin would have the ultimate send-off.

We created a two week parade of love. As friends and family eagerly lined up to share their favorite memories, we laughed until we cried. I watched Kelli's eyes light up, with every face who entered her room, and I was certain she finally knew how much she was truly loved and not just someone to pity. I also felt the sadness in her heart as reality crept in. The bittersweetness of knowing that what she had waited to feel her entire life, would soon be coming to an end.

On the morning of my cousins last day on earth, as she lay deep in a medicated coma, I had a vision from my Grandma Jo, at the perfect opportunity to deliver the message. I knew Kelli was painfully resisting her release from this world, mostly because she had no real faith in where she was going and was terrified to leave. Regardless of the years she had spent parroting spiritual words, or sitting in congregations with those who rarely practice what they preach, Kelli could only see death as the dark and fearful unknown.

Now, as I sat holding her nearly lifeless hand, I whispered in Kelli's ear about the new world where she would be going in order to help create a more loving humanity, a place that can only survive through the energy of light, beauty, peace, and joy. I let her know I could already see her spirit gleefully riding on the backs of the most radiant wild horses, galloping along the ocean shore. I excitedly encouraged her to let her tired body rest, so she could start this brand new adventure, an experience of blissful peace, in another dimension, where all souls unite in the energy of love.

I encouraged Kelli to imagine her idea of heaven and the most magical dream she wouldn't want to wake up from. I promised that I would be right by her side until she was greeted by all of her guardian angels and every loved one she wanted to see. At the end of my promise, I saw a tear fall from her eye, and two hours later she released her soul to fly home. That was our last time together on this planet. The scene that played out during her final breaths, went exactly as I had described to her. Surrounded by loved ones, with me whispering in her ear, coaching her through. I am firmly convinced, after endless conversations and worrying that all my efforts might have fallen on deaf ears, I know she heard every word I said—and always did.

To date, I have witnessed more deaths than births. Without hesitation, I know and believe that each soul knows their divine journey and greater purpose for being here. Why does it seem that the good die so young? If you can observe the truth of their soul, you will know they chose the perfect ending that matched their strongest beliefs, lifestyle choices, and greater purpose for being here. The example of one life, no matter how long, may be all that's needed to impact thousands, elevating humanity to higher levels of vibration.

Where did we get the idea that if we do not live for a hundred years, that means we were robbed of time or didn't do something right? Who among us has the authority to decide what is a miracle or a mistake? A blessing or a curse? A tragedy or the catalyst for greater transformation? Can you begin to see how even a newborn baby, who has a much older and wiser soul, knows exactly what their reason for being is? Living a good life has nothing to do with the number of candles on a birthday cake.

When you really think about it, the most valuable and limited commodity we have in the human experience, is time. Unfortunately, many of us, myself included, often make time our enemy. When we are young, we can't wait to grow up and when we grow up, we just want to be a kid again. Many people spend their entire lives trying to beat the clock, or wishing they could slow it down. They regret the time they spend noticing and complaining about every pound, wrinkle, sag, ache, and pain as we age; the time they spend worrying about the unknown and everything out of our control; the time they spend attempting to escape an unwanted reality; the time they spend in battle with their own thoughts and emotions, or with others'; the time they spend chasing external validation, money, and material possessions; the time they spend second guessing and talking themselves out of their own dreams.

We regret the time we spend in relationships that do more harm than good; the time we spend missing our loved ones; the time we spend living a life based on other people's needs and wants; the time we spend in work that doesn't please our soul; the time we spend fueling toxic negativity that ultimately destroys our health and quality of life; the time we spend believing we don't have enough time.

The bottom line is that the sooner you make time your friend, and not your enemy, the healthier your life will be. Stop resisting change or, on the flipside, pushing for change to occur before the most appropriate and beneficial timing. Learn how to be in the present and you will have all the time in the world. Just as when you naturally formed in your mother's womb, you didn't stress if you had all of your fingers and toes, or about when you would be making your grand entrance. You were comfortably unaware and content in the naturalness of amnio. Believe it or not, you still have the ability to begin anew in the same organic flow of nothing but love. Allowing the attitude of complete joy and abundance, in all facets, to easily become your reality.

Always remember, life is not happening to you, it is responding to you. The most beneficial way to let this work in your favor is to stop "doing" so much in the physical world of action, and start "being" the best version of you in every single day. When you stop trying to control the world, and everyone in it, you will then have far more time to do what you love—leaving no room for drama or stressful nonsense. Your only job is to focus on anything and everything that feels good when you think about it. If you struggle to find very much that inspires or excites you, then it's clearly time to become selfish enough to get there. The more fun you have, the easier it is to let go of everything you don't enjoy.

The ultimate human experience is when you have positively aligned yourself with the energy of universal time. What we label as good or bad memories can be revisited in just a few thoughts, whether it happened yesterday or years ago, we can relive it in a moment's notice. Therefore, the calendar and the clock are not your best compass, you are.

Our bodies are simply a house for our spirit. If you don't take care of your home, it will become dilapidated beyond repair, leaving the soul no choice but to fly away from it. The cold hard truth is, chronic illness and terminal death sentences do not appear out of nowhere, nor from an unlucky fate. When we refuse to listen to our wakeup calls, or make our own wellbeing a priority, we will live and die in ways which completely reflect our choices. The physical outcomes take on different names, depending on the area affected, but it all begins as unhealthy energy that eventually manifests from the inside out. All the signs and symptoms that rise to the surface are an indication of greater distress inside. For Kelli, it was her own thoughts, and corresponding emotional upheaval, that were her greatest source of unease, or dis-ease, eventually weakening her mind and her entire body. Sadly, most humans repeatedly ignore the minor annoyances, until they are faced with a major crisis, with no simple options.

You need to know that the possibility of a long and happy life lies within the alignment of mind, body, and soul, living in positive belief and the energy of love. The powerless can gain tremendous strength in belief of a power greater than ourselves, more usually believed to be the judge and jury of our destiny. However, the idea that there is a puppet master in the sky and we are all just helpless puppets, makes for a limited and fearful existence at best. The most healing energy in the universe, is accessible within us all.

Regardless of who or what you believe to be the ultimate authority, you will always need to take full ownership for your own free will and choices. You will only live a problematic life when you are always consumed with so called "problems." Spend more time focused on all that is going well, instead of negative concerns. Again, this doesn't mean you must live in denial, it means that you quickly acknowledge any warning signs and speed bumps as opportunities to slow you down and guide you back to safety.

I have observed enough with myself and my own loved ones, as well as having a thorough understanding of the Law of Attraction, to make the following bold statements: The truth is, every mental and physical illness is simply a growing disconnection from the love and truth of the soul/spirit. The buildup of energy as a result of holding too much anger, blame, resentment, guilt, fear, worry, hurt, sadness, and grief is toxic.

The more you fuel anything that doesn't feel good, the more damage you will do to your mind and/or body. Regardless of the area of your aches and pains, or medical reason for them, there is always an interrelated link between the thoughts we choose to believe are true about us, and how this impacts our mind, body and overall experience.

People will often turn to pills, drugs, alcohol, or food, for relief, often to unhealthy extremes and even life threatening proportions, all as a method of medicating and numbing the pain of the mind and body, never really touching the true source of the discomfort.

We want to believe letters behind names will signify the knowledge and comfort we can trust, but this is not always the case. We will only need medical assistance when we have allowed ourselves to get too far out of alignment from self-care and positive belief. The healing energy of your own love is the most organic medicine in the universe.

The ultimate guide to health is listening to the truth of your own mind, body, and spirit. Basically, our entire anatomy is set up to respond to the signals of the brain. When we have an itch, our mind sends the signal to the hand to scratch it. We will only crave, and become addicted to, something that we have habitually digested and trained our mind and body to obsessively and compulsively expect. Our bodies can become so dependent, on a chemical that we can become deathly ill without it.

Especially as we age, the fewer foreign substances and manufactured medicines our bodies have to figure out what to do with, the better. If we believe we have a disability or handicap, the body will forever follow accordingly. If you believe there is something wrong with you, or if you spend time worrying there will be, eventually you will prove yourself right. I would encourage anyone who is dealing with some sort of health issue, especially if it is currently affecting your quality of life, to immediately get to the core of the negative energy creating the discomfort. I know it's easy to focus on the presenting issues, however they will soon subside when your commitment to feeling better is stronger. The unhealthiest members of society become that way from a distorted belief system and a nervous system fueled by fear. The most tortured will suffer in the false beliefs that they were born malfunctioned, and cursed for life. This just isn't true.

There is only one way into this world, and one way out. What you need in the physical world is exactly what you were born with, nothing except a naked body full of love. Everything of true value, just like you, begins and ends with unconditional love. Fill your days with positive and productive action, in the direction of what you want. There is a rhyme and reason for it all, don't get so bogged down in the details that you lose sight of the bigger picture.

If you want to "fight" your way through anything, I would encourage everyone to conquer the urge to think, say or do anything that does not offer pleasing emotions within. Believe it or not, and regardless of the name you give it, there is a very powerful and positive flowing stream of well-being that we are all a part of. We will only strain and struggle when we attempt to go in the opposite direction of what we know is truly best for us.

To honor my love and promise to Kelli, and all others who want their story to be the difference for those in need of healing assistance, I tell you this: you are the one who decides your attitude, and game face, no matter what hand you're dealt. No one walks through this life without being knocked down a time or two. The sooner you marshal your own strength to lift yourself up, the faster you will realize nothing and no one can overpower you again. Regardless of the conditions or current state of health, your attitude will determine every outcome. A healthy lifestyle goes way beyond diet and exercise, a healthy lifestyle is mostly about how you choose to think and feel about yourself. Choose wisely and get well soon.

Chapter 7: From Seven Sins to Seventh Heaven

Can you guess the number one factor at the heart of vanity, greed, lust, envy, gluttony, wrath, and sloth? Contrary to popular opinion, arrogance is not a sign of confidence, boasting is not a sign of high self-esteem, and aggression is not a sign of courage. If anything, those comparisons are actually on opposite ends of the spectrum. The sins of humanity are always grounded in a mentality of lack, fear, and insecurity; the real "devil" in the details.

A disempowered mind will seek to justify, rationalize, excuse, convince, manipulate, persuade, possess, bully, dominate, and control. An empowered mind will seek harmony, unity, integrity, honesty, generosity, and simplicity. The path of least resistance does not mean the easiest and fastest route to get ahead. The road to fortune is found in the awareness that abundance comes easily and frequently when you are in full belief of this truth.

One of the most common driving factors across the globe, is money. The myths about wealth fall somewhere in between the root of all evil and the measure of success. The sin is in believing that our personal value is equal to our net worth. How do you put a price tag on the worth of each soul? How do you determine which gifts and talents are worth millions and which only deserve pennies? How do you appreciate complete abundance without the fear that it will be taken away?

Unfortunately, a posh and lavish lifestyle has become the standard of excellence, as well as a way to incite the envy and animosity of the seemingly less fortunate. What most have witnessed in their lifetime, is the rich shall, in fact, inherit the earth and the meek shall also get walked on to get there. There is factual evidence that the smallest percentage of the world's population hold almost all of the wealth, leaving the bulk of humanity baffled, scratching their heads, and scrambling for lucky numbers, or searching for the Wizard who can lead them to the Emerald City.

The common thread, in the emperor's clothes, is not sewn by luck, fate, destiny, favor, or even inheritance. The secret to success is in the expectation of your belief or lack thereof. For example, statistics show us that many people who win the lottery squander their entire winnings within a few years and are often left in worse shape than before they won. Why? They had full belief they would win, but they didn't necessarily have belief in their ability to make it last. Money doesn't buy a new way of thinking or behaving.

What we need to understand, and to know, is that money, in and of itself, has no value other than what the people decide. The economy is continually fluctuating according to the vibration of greater consciousness across the planet. Why would we ever link our happiness or security to something so volatile and out of our control? We have witnessed humans lie, cheat, steal, kill, or take their own lives, over money; which is truly nothing more than paper and metal.

Most people have a love/hate relationship with money depending on the core messages they were raised with. For instance, I grew up in a lower middle class family of manual laborers who worked very hard for very little pay. As the oldest of three kids, I started finding ways to make my own money as soon as I could. I bought my own school clothes and anything else that really mattered to me, usually presents for other people.

Although being raised with very little disposable income is exactly what made me the independent, resourceful, and driven person I am. At the same time, I would never allow myself to rise too far above the bar of family pride and loyalty. The underlying message I heard loud and clear, spoken or unspoken, was that wealthy people were the enemy. Time and time again, it was pointed out that rich people thought they were better than those who didn't have very much, which I knew meant us.

In my confusion and sadness, I could still see the hunger in my loved ones eyes every time they talked about having more for themselves. It was as if somehow only a chosen few were given the map to all of the gold, and the rest of us were be forced to go without. Even more disturbing, I was given to understand that they were too selfish to share. I wondered how numbers behind a dollar sign could ever make someone think they mattered more than anyone else. I decided early that if money made you become someone like that, then I never wanted to have more than I needed to survive.

The double-edged sword was that I also saw the lure of having means and a way to nice things and the life of my dreams. Therefore, I always seemed to find myself in a pattern of climbing my way out of nothing, only to fail when I was so close to what I wanted. Sabotaging my own financial success every time.

Any time we set limits on our potential or worthiness, it doesn't feel good because we are holding ourselves back from who we really are. The truth is, if we are inspired to visualize the dream, we also have the ability to create the manifestation. Our universe is extremely generous and holds an unlimited amount of treasures and experiences to please and satisfy everyone in it. However, there will never be enough money to change your mind—especially about money. The path to eternal abundance is an inside job and the payoff is priceless.

Do you believe there is enough for everyone to have it all? Do you believe it's possible for you? Life is not a game to see who can outsmart time as you race for the pot of gold, fountain of youth, or perfect partner. There is no conspiracy working against you to take your fair share, or hold you back from anything. There is absolutely no one you have to compete with, or compare yourself to. Nor does anyone owe you anything. There is no shortage of health, wealth, or happiness in this infinitely abundant universe.

If you make decisions based solely on feeding your ego, you will live a superficial and shallow existence at best. These goals may include, but are not limited to, the following: physical appearance, money, sex, fame, image, possessions, popularity, or feeding any other insecurities. When you first learn to stay true to your free spirit and do what you love, there is no need to look for the right person, place, or thing that will do that for you. The universal truth, the Law of Attraction, will show you the perfect path, and partners, every time.

The bottom line is that you don't need a truckload of 100 dollar bills to be dumped in your driveway or a "Sugar Momma/Daddy" to pay your way. There are many that will choose this disempowering and detrimental path but they are only declaring a lack of full belief in self-reliance. We will never have the tools and skills to create an amazing life if we are only waiting for a hand out, or seeking someone willing to take care of us.

A healthy respect for the laws of the universe will take anyone from rags to riches, turning desperation into inspiration. If you attach power or meaning to anything in the material world, you are forever at the mercy of your chosen "Ruler/God." Attempting to fit into a life of someone else's design, will ultimately leave you feeling empty and unsatisfied.

Instead, I propose you notice the many natural gifts and abilities you already hold within, and allow them to rise to the surface. Have as much fun as possible as you follow your natural interests and intrigue from the inside out. It doesn't mean that people will automatically start throwing money at you overnight. Although, when you are feeling in love with what you are doing, you are in the same vibration as complete abundance and the power to create worlds. Let the universe do the heavy lifting while you take time to align with the benefit of you, and all you have become.

*"Just as every butterfly will emerge
from a protective cocoon, you too have been
preparing to be free. Transforming in the darkness
to know the strength and courage of your soul.
Ready to spread your beautiful wings and fly
into the bliss of sunlight."*

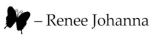 – Renee Johanna

Chapter 8: **Let Go and Let Love**

The most difficult part of change is not the awareness of what needs to be done, it's the doing of it. The big question is always HOW? How do I turn my attention to something other than what I am experiencing right now, in my current reality, and in the world around me? How can I possibly speak my truth and risk hurting someone I love? How can I feel powerful when I have forever felt like a victim? How do I honor my own life and release the need to please everyone else?

The underlying answer to everything is really very simple but we all make it unnecessarily complicated. I can see from my own experience, as well as everything I have ever heard, read, or witnessed in others; there is always one recurring source of wisdom and strength since the beginning of time. Drumroll, please................... LOVE!

Without exception, love is the purest form of energy that creates the most positive results, every time. Love is the source of all creation; the solution to every problem and the magical way forward for all. No matter the religion, culture, nationality, spirituality, or skepticism, there will always exist the universal language of love. What we can see, touch, hear, smell, and taste, is always so much better when fueled with the positive energy of love. Expressed and experienced in multiple ways, to please the human senses. Love is an ultimate and inclusive energy, which connects every soul to another.

The hurt and heartbreak, falsely associated with love, is in the impossible illusion that this energy is selective. Just as with the air we breathe, love cannot be captured or confined, given or taken away. It is an invisible energy that naturally flows to you and through you, truly oxygen for the soul. Love is not ruled by time, space or physical conditions but is perfectly managed by the universal law of attraction.

The HOW part of this process begins from the inside out. When you make the commitment to stop doing anything and everything that doesn't feel good to you. Listen to the wisest part of you, the intuition of your soul, and align with the highest vibration of love. When you follow through with this guidance, you build more trust and confidence in yourself. The more belief you have in you, the easier it is to create a life of your dreams.

Offer yourself the most positive messages you can believe about yourself in the present, and set no limits to your future. Stop waiting for someday, or someone, and start searching for more ways to access what you want right now. Continually offer healthy, positive, choices for your body, mind, and soul. Treat yourself with kindness and respect since this is the template you set for how other people will treat you.

No matter how many different relationships you have in place right now, the most important one is with yourself. You can instantly receive the benefit of positive emotions, anytime you notice or think about something that pleases you. The connection grows when you have quality time alone to positively reflect and expand on your mental list of even more things to love. Seek any opportunity to feel alive and apart of all that is. In such complete harmony and satisfaction in the moment, time seems to stand still.

It is important to remember that when you are in a state of love and appreciation, whatever the reason, you are in positive alignment with the source of you—pure love. This is exactly how you love yourself. When you are finding more and more reasons to laugh and smile, you are loving yourself. When you are doing things that you genuinely enjoy, you are loving yourself. When you are feeling love for others, you are loving yourself. When you are treating yourself as your best friend, and not your worst enemy, you are loving yourself.

Quite frankly, if you don't appreciate and enjoy your time alone with you, why would anyone else? Each one of us is far more fun and attractive when we are feeling our best and vibrating that positive energy from the inside out. Stop looking for love in all the wrong places. Get right with you first, and then you will feel loved beyond belief.

Be less concerned about who's by your side, or if others are loving and appreciating you enough. Focus on what you actually have control of: you. Give yourself a permanent break from any self-criticism and let everyone else off the hook as well. Commit to falling in love with your own life first, and then choose the people you want to share it with and to what degree.

On the way to awakening, we can assign a variety of conditions, judgments, expectations, rules, and requirements about life; often in the name of love. However, the true bliss of this magic carpet ride is actually experienced as you release the need to control it. When you can let go and let love, you are truly a free spirit.

Where do you start? Let go of anything and everything that does not support or create a feeling of empowerment. This includes:

- Watching, reading, discussing the news, politics, religion, etc. Whether it's local, national or international, we will save ourselves a lot of time and wasted energy as the news is, by far, more negative over positive anyway. Unless the most current news is directly related to your safety and survival, any relevant news pertaining to your personal growth and development will be brought to your attention at the right time.

- Participating in gossip/negative discussion of anyone's story, drama, troubles, or misery, even if you know if it's actually true or not. This is not the way to understanding and will only create additional chaos in your own life. Any input, in the absence of that party, should be in their defense and only what you love and/or appreciate about them.

- Negative self-talk, mentally beating the bleep out of ourselves over and over is never going to get us better but will make us get much worse, and very quickly. Regardless of what we have said or done in the past, now is the time to release the demons we may still keep hidden.

Criticism serves no purpose but to keep us trapped in a prison of punishment.

Complete self-love and awareness means you are willing to embrace the truth. Courageously taking a deeper look at the good, the bad, the ugly, and everything in between (even though it is all divinely perfect and beautiful). Discover how to use love and compassion to heal any emotional wounds, rather than ignoring and making them fester, just like a nurturing mother who reassures a hurt child to play again, after kissing the booboo and making it better.

We cannot truly be free of unwanted painful memories until we allow a safe and loving place in our psyche to lay them to rest. The internal transformation from a critical fear-based mind, to one of ultimate self-care and love, does not happen overnight. However, with a steady commitment to do whatever it takes to feel better and better, each new day brings a brighter light to follow, eventually ending our sob stories, once and for all.

Each human is born with the same natural ability to continually access a better version of yourself. You will become your wisest teacher and eager student all at the same time, the objective observer inside, who is always ready to for you to expand into higher and higher levels of awareness. You will be awake and aligned with all you intended to be, do, and have while here on earth.

We can become extremely lost and confused in our minds but the purest version of who we really are, and our connection to the source of love, can never be lost completely. Whenever we hold ourselves away from the gravitational pull of positive energy, we will experience the mental, emotional, physical and even spiritual opposite of what we desire. No matter the degree of disconnect, we will always be drawn back to an experience of feeling whole, as well as a part of something bigger than just ourselves.

We all are our own best friend, our loudest cheerleader and loyal fan, who always has our best interest at heart. Our most accurate guide who never stops reminding us what feels good and what doesn't. The one who loves and supports you no matter what. The biggest part of you who loves unconditionally.

Many of us may have stopped listening to our highest self a long time ago. We allowed the beliefs, opinions and validation from others to become more important than our own truth. We either conformed to, or rebelled against, the ones who attempted to control our spirit. Either way, we gave another personality the power over our guide, which is our own intuition.

This is why it is imperative to focus on managing self, first and foremost. When we truly commit to feeling love from the inside out, as our top priority, we become more soul-centered and less-ego driven. Approaching life and all creation from a positive mental and emotional state, we become the best example for everyone around us to do the same. In this pattern we move from self-centered, to self-loved, to soul love, which only knows equality and eternal love for one and all.

The most effective and quickest route from pain to peace is through focus on kindness and caring for self. This less traveled road also happens to be the path of least resistance. Patients heal faster and may even outlive a death sentence the more they focus on what they love and appreciate. Relationships flourish and thrive longer the more both parties are living as their highest self. Miracles happen every day through the powerful energy of love.

Following are several ways to begin incorporating habits of self-care. The more we focus our attention on subjects that empower, enlighten and inspire us while implementing new behaviors that correspond, any self-defeating habits will naturally be eliminated completely. Self-love and self-hate cannot live in the same body. Choose which method works best for you and build your own template as you go.

- Create a list of positive attributes about you as well as what you love to see as you look outside of you. Find the most uplifting thoughts, believable to you, and continue looking for ways to add to them. For example: today I can choose whatever attitude I want to have; all of my needs are being met and I know this is true because I'm still breathing; today I am one step closer to seeing my dreams become a physical reality; today anything is possible as it is a clean slate of intention; today I love having people and experiences in my life which can show me more of who I am.

- Every morning, when you wake and before you leave your bed, repeat your list of positive attributes/mantras/affirmations/visions that generate the best feeling energy running through you. This will set the tone for your entire day.

- Seek as much information as possible that helps you understand the Law of Attraction and the universal guidance already in operation. This information should stretch your thinking in a way that offers a positive connection to what you are receiving without confusion. As you seek, more teachers will show up.

- Allow time every day for your senses to be stimulated in a healthy way and just for you through: music, dancing, art, entertainment, laughter, fun, passions, hobbies, or pampering.

- Choose healthier options for your body and reduce anything unhealthy until eliminated: food, drink, and anything else you take in. Preventative maintenance is key to managing your health.

- Do exercise/a physical activity you enjoy more times throughout your week than not.

- Surround yourself with people who are optimistic, open minded, supportive, and self-aware enough to keep their priority of focus on their own good feeling energy.

- Allow all other people, especially your loved ones, their own path to self-discovery and happiness. Always bring the internal focus back to you as you learn to emotionally detach with love and picture them only in their brightest light, no matter their current struggle. You are of much better service to others when you are in a good feeling place yourself.

- Allow love and laughter to fill any gaps inside of you. Do not resist a kind word or a loving gesture.

- Get lost in meditation (meditation is any process that helps you align with source energy and divine oneness) as often as possible. Breathe, release, and center with love. There is no wrong way to meditate but the goal is always in the direction of being still enough to create a feeling of calm. There are multiple resources to guide you until you master this on your own: listening to calming music, guided imagery, and more.

- Practice, Practice, Practice! There are no perfect humans, but there is perfection in the process of allowing your soul to be free in the human experience. We are never done learning, growing, and expanding. Be kind, gentle, and patient, with you, as you learn to enjoy this journey and the joyful adventure you always knew it would be.

The strongest foundation, in order to continually offer yourself strength in the face of fear, is always making your mental and emotional state of wellbeing top priority. No matter what you believe demands your attention in your waking moments, you are of no good to anyone when you are not good to yourself. Diligently generating thoughts that feel good as you think them, can shift your entire perspective. Allowing the clarity to see life from a much more enlightened and happier perspective.

Your list can never be too long in the direction of love and appreciation. You are the only one who determines, from the minute you wake up, what kind of day you are going to have. We have a choice to keep reliving the past, whether it was yesterday or 20 years ago, or stay grounded in the present. We have a choice to repeat history or move confidently into a brighter tomorrow, with all that we know now.

Too difficult you say? The truth is that it is more difficult to live in a world that does not allow for love to be the beginning, the end and everything in between. It is actually more difficult to stay in a relationship that no longer feels good, but the fear of the unknown is greater than what's known. It is more difficult to continue an addictive habit but fear you will never feel better or free without it. It is agonizing to do work that doesn't please your soul, but you see too many obstacles keeping you from what you would really love to do. It is torture to spend your days suffering in physical and psychic pain believing you are hopeless and helpless to experience anything better for yourself.

Is it still hard to believe that all of this is possible for everyone including you? If the answer is yes, it simply means you have not yet personally connected to a deeper appreciation of yourself through the eyes of source/love. This is what many refer to as a Spiritual Awakening. I like to call it the process of falling in love with your own soul, when the human/ego and the spirit/soul harmonically combine as one divine entity. When you can open your mind and heart to allow the transfusion of pure loving energy to run through our veins, this is all that is needed to create everlasting happiness.

It is never too late for anyone to wake up to their personal power. However, nothing changes if nothing changes. We will keep getting the same results, and feeling the same way if we continue thinking, speaking, and acting in the same ways which produce those outcomes. Instead, you can make a commitment every day, to a deliberate practice of thinking, speaking, and acting in ways that make you feel better and better about you.

We are each offered a fresh canvas to paint a new picture every day. We can rewrite our story any time we choose. The current circumstances of our lives are just a result of previous thoughts put in motion. Other people, or events, do not determine our current happiness or our value, only we do. Let go and let love, all others will follow your lead.

Chapter 9: The Ultimate Mindset

This is an exciting era to be alive and experiencing life on this planet. Never before have we had such a massive acceleration of technology in a relatively, short amount of time. We basically have the ability to connect to anyone or anything at our fingertips. Sadly, all of this focus and progress, on inventions and solutions to extend our lives in the most convenient ways, has taken no time at all in comparison to the development and expectation of the human character.

There are many who have already awakened and are exploring this new environment and seeking to feel even more alive and in joyful new ways. This "re-birth" can happen at any time, at any age, and for any number of reasons. Typically, a Spiritual Awakening will follow a period of what most describe as the darkest period of their life. A suffocating blanket becomes the cape of our super human strength and the catalyst for our greatest transformation.

Those milestone moments in time when we hit the final bottom of our personal hell and decide we have experienced enough sadness, grief, anger, rage, fear, terror, pain, sickness, suffering, self-pity, guilt, blame, resentment, denial, hurt, confusion, self-loathing, disgust, hate, or ignorance… to last a life time. We choose to no longer live in a land of lies, and will go to any lengths just to be who we genuinely are—a free spirit once and for all.

We also know many more people who are still asleep. These are the people I refer to as "sleepwalkers." They are oblivious to the concept that they are the ones who are creating their dreams as well as their nightmares. Their focus is either on the past, or in the future, but rarely fully engaged in the present. More importance is placed on outside influence and opinion than the truth within. They believe only in what they see—yet what they see is just a glimpse at the big picture.

We can attempt to gently nudge or even violently shake another to wake up from their self-imposed limitations. However, until they are completely ready for a higher level of awareness, there is really nothing we can say or do which will create that desire for them. Living our truth in the positive proof of our own lives is the best example for any other.

Now that I realize I have absolutely lived in two very different worlds in one lifetime, I can clearly see that I was awake this entire time. However, without a comfortable awareness or direction, I kept trying to put myself back to sleep. Most of my waking moments were pure torture, as I had no idea why I felt the passionate desire to save a world that I really didn't want to be in. Little did I know that my reason for being here is the same reason I wanted to leave. I could only help others through my own experience.

At this point, you will continue to observe, replace, and release many old beliefs that no longer work for you. As you shift your thoughts, words, and actions, you will quickly receive universal feedback, especially from your friends and family. People who know you well will start pointing out that there is "something different" about you. All these responses are positive validation that you are on the right path.

You must always aim for your character to be bigger than your circumstance. Choose to see every so called "problem" currently in your reality as just another opportunity for a better version of you to show up this time. It will become easier to emotionally detach from a belief system that no longer serves you, when you practice becoming an impartial and joyous observer of your own life. It allows you to explore your options from a calmer perspective, through the eyes of love and well-being for all, rather than impulsively reacting from negative emotions.

The only thing you need to do right now is to decide how you want to feel about a certain subject and what you can do to support that emotional experience. The following is a perfect model of the most successful and empowering mindset you can develop as well as the polar opposite characteristics of fear based thinking.

Positive Mindset vs. Negative Mindset

Abundance	Lack/Not Enough
Prosperity	Scarcity
Optimistic	Pessimistic
Can Do	Can't Do
Confident	Doubtful
Courageous	Fearful
Growth focused	Fixed Based/Status Quo
Bold/Assertive	Timid/Passive
Calm/Peaceful	Nervous/Anxious
Kind/Thoughtful	Mean/Rude
Loving	Hateful
Generous	Stingy/Greedy
Giver/Servant	Self-Consumed
Appreciative/Thankful	Ungrateful
Trusting	Distrustful
Honest	Dishonest
Purposeful	Directionless
Adaptive	Resistant
Resourceful	Helpless
Soul/Strength Based	Ego/Flaw Based
Open Minded	Closed Minded
Aware/Awake	Unaware/Asleep
Visionary/Leader	Confused/Follower
Creator	Victim

Embracing each positive element in this list can create the ultimate mindset and optimum emotional well-being. This is the most beneficial strategy to manifest desirable life experiences further expanding your infinite potentiality and the unlimited abundance of prosperity, wealth, health, love and happiness available to you right now. You simply need to acknowledge, understand, embrace, develop, and maintain a constant state of allowance and appreciation for what you know to be true now.

Get the idea? We really do have a choice in our attitude and which trait we prefer to apply to any situation we are presented with. The more we practice the qualities of a positive mindset, the more favorable the outcomes in every area of our life. Operating from a predominately fearful and negative mindset, is inviting more to join in the pity party of misery. The only thing we really ever need to change, in order to experience the abundance of good feeling energy, is our own mind.

It is impossible to have a positive mindset and a negative mindset occurring simultaneously. We are either focused on what we want or what we don't want; what we like or what we don't like; what we have or what we don't have. According to universal law, dual energies (also known as polarities or opposites), cannot exist together in harmonic combination, blowing the theory that opposites attract.

When you are experiencing great appreciation about yourself and your life, keep doing what you are doing, and be open to even better. When you are experiencing confusion and overwhelming emotion, it is an indication that you are in a downward spiral of disempowering beliefs. You will need to do what works best for you to get centered and positively redirected as soon as possible.

For example, you have just been told about a new opportunity opening up at the perfect time that will allow you to do what you love. You have the choice to think thoughts of doubt and negative "what ifs," or you can choose to respond to this news immediately with thoughts of appreciation and well-deserved validation. You can even have a combination of many positive and negative responses, however, the dominating thoughts you agree with will impact your outcome tremendously.

Which thoughts feel better to you? Statements of doubts and limitations: what if this is too good to be true? what if I make this decision and it was a mistake? what if I'm not ready and I fail? what if I don't make enough money? what if I get my hopes up and then get disappointed? Or statements of positive belief: I can see my efforts starting to show up in new opportunities; I know even more amazing events will come my way as I focus and become clearer and clearer about what I want; I am excited that there are many paths to happiness and I only need to follow the path that feels like the best fit for what I want for myself right now.

Notice the contrast in energy from doubt to trust. More self-empowering statements build a strong momentum of encouraging, supportive, and positively validating thoughts. This will always feel uplifting on the inside because you are feeding your soul. When you are tapped into love, joy, and appreciation, you have access to an ocean of manifestations.

On the other hand, a strong momentum of fear-based thoughts will feel very uncomfortable because this conflicts with the wisdom of your highest self. If you continue to let your fear have control, it will eventually produce at least one or many, physical symptoms to get your attention such as anxiety, depression, mental and physical illnesses, ailments, aches, pains, and diseases. In an effort to protect yourself from further disappointment and discomfort, you misguidedly discourage yourself from moving in the very direction that will offer exactly what you want and need.

I strongly encourage you to put all of your focus and emotional energy in to creating and implementing your most advantageous mindset. Over time, you will eliminate your existing limited mind. Typically you will struggle with some traits more than others depending how ingrained the habit and belief are.

The purpose of all of this work, is not to become perfect or never have a negative thought or emotion again. The objective is to become aware of which mindset, positive or negative, you habitually gravitate to, and whether this thinking is serving your highest good or not. Regardless of the situation or circumstance, it always comes down to how you want to feel about it. Simplified, the desire for positive emotions and outcomes will require a positive mindset.

Most humans forget that they have free will. Instead, they turn to false beliefs that some are just born with the good/right stuff, and some are not. The truth is that we all arrive on earth with exactly what we need; a bare body; a mind to imagine and create our reality; and an emotional guidance system to keep us on track. The rest of what we need is a perfect combination of other beings, places, and things to help us grow and evolve in this world. We are just as our soul intended—free to be, do, and love in the human experience.

As you continue a daily practice of operating from a positive mindset, you will activate ongoing attractive energy to you, and it will flow through you. You will naturally start to desire health and wellbeing, choosing feeling good as your top priority at all times. You will see yourself excitedly participating in the making of your own dreams. You will confidently trust your intuition and enjoy greater knowing of what's best for you. In the heart of each set of eyes you connect with you will see beauty and love first. You will be the inspiration to uplift and encourage all others who want the same for themselves.

It will benefit you immensely to make a thorough and honest evaluation of which side, in the set of traits above, you currently gravitate toward in your day to day to life. Acknowledge each one, and its opposite, as you identify with the examples of your life. Is there a disconnection between what you want to believe is true, and what you know is true right now?

Remember, your current beliefs are just an accumulation of past thoughts stored in your memory bank. What you previously labeled as good and bad or right and wrong, does not matter to the universal mind. What is of utmost importance is to be aware of the most beneficial thoughts you can believe right now, shifting your current mindset in order to accurately guide yourself into the future you desire.

For example, between Abundance and Lack, do you always focus on appreciation of all you have right now? Do you know that even more will show up for you, and everyone else, as you stay in positive alignment with receiving what you believe? Or does your attention more often gravitate to what's missing, what you're worried about, and feeling the discomfort of not enough?

When you think of Prosperity vs. Scarcity, do you believe the potential exists for all to succeed and prosper, including you? Or do you believe there is a limited supply/access of opportunity for all? Do you believe you are the creator of all experiences that you receive, or do you believe you can still be a victim in certain circumstances?

You can feel overwhelmed and frustrated if you expect to jump from a limited mind to an empowered one overnight. The entire process of transformation will be much easier and more fun if you feel your way through this change, as opposed to spinning in thought. Gently and patiently incorporate the next set of traits and practices as you are ready. This will allow you to feel better and better each day, instead of pushing yourself through these changes.

Building your own ultimate mindset means the race is over and everybody wins. There is no value/benefit to you, or anyone else, to fuel traits in the negative mindset. As we embrace and incorporate each positive element, in every area of our life, the negative counterpart will naturally subside and eventually become barely visible in our reality.

Have I convinced you yet? Well, be prepared to have your mind blown as we explore every aspect of creating amazing human experiences from the inside out. We will see the common links to be able to incorporate an ultimate mindset, in every avenue of life: relationships, work, money, health, etc. Ready? The fun has just begun!

Chapter 10: A Life of Passion and Purpose

Every day, I have the incredible pleasure of conversing with leading edge minds from all over the world. One of the biggest thrills for me is when I can witness another person tap into their own fire.

As someone who has spent a ridiculous amount of my life pretending to be just like everyone else constantly hiding who I was naturally, I have committed the rest of my days to save precious time for others. After exhausting my search for the road to riches using a broken compass, I finally gave myself permission to just be me, beyond ready to be free to do what I love forever and let the chips fall where they may.

The majority of the working population are still echoing the same disdain of dissatisfaction, "if only I could be blessed enough to do what I love and be able to pay the bills at the same time." There are far too many who are still not living a life of their own design, and who are unsure in their ability to create it. Sadly, there are too many people who have completely given up on the idea of falling in love with life and are barely motivated to function through their days.

Many people choose the route of obtaining an enormous amount of education and advice in order to make the "right" decisions for the future, eager to develop the perfect plan to achieve their dreams and a life of abundance, hopefully generating more than enough money to feed their bodies, minds, and souls.

Without a doubt, there is beneficial information in the proven and possible. Seeking additional insight from the success of another is never a bad thing. However, there will never be a better guidance and direction than first aligning with what feeds your own soul.

How do you know how to achieve this alignment? A great place to start is by noticing what you tend to gravitate to for personal pleasure right now—those times when you feel the greatest sense of satisfaction within. The path of least resistance is typically what comes so natural to you, and it can easily be overlooked and unappreciated as anything special, let alone a gift or calling.

Discovering the direction that will allow and enhance your passion and purpose, is much easier than people realize. If you take a closer look at what you are excitedly drawn to and excel at already, you will get the bulk of your answers. What happens to most people, especially if they have fulfilled the same role for multiple years, is a tendency to set aside their other interests for so long that they forget about them. Regardless, of your current obligations or limitations, now is the perfect time to prepare for the rest of your dreams to become reality.

Before reading one more "how to get rich quick" book or taking one more workshop by the latest motivational guru, please take the time to be just with you. Notice what genuinely brings you joy, excitement, fun, passion, attraction, intrigue, meaning, connection, and curiosity on a daily basis. Explore and incorporate multiple methods to align your mind with positive energy.

Just as you could never plan an amazing trip without first deciding where you really want to go, you need to acknowledge the truth of your intentions, interests, and excitement before choosing the appropriate direction to your destination. When you can own and appreciate your own natural gifts and abilities, you have the perfect starting point to choose any avenue that will nurture your development most as your highest and best self.

There are several techniques and tools to assist you in this process. I have already listed many in the previous pages. The key is to build your program of wellness to suit you. Personally, I am a huge fan of meditation above all else. (Except for reading this book over and over… of course). I also realize that the reason most people resist the idea of meditation is because they may have tried it once or twice and found no value in it. Possibly they were even left feeling more frustrated or fearful than before they did it. In all actuality, the goal of completely shutting your mind down seems impossible, because it is.

Meditation is not about reaching a level of brain death so you can leave your body. In my experience, it is more like an incredible therapeutic massage for the mind, body, and soul at once. At the very least, it will offer a reprieve from any internal crap and clutter, allowing the purest energy to flow through you like fresh oxygen, much like napping or a good night's rest.

Meditating as little as 10 or 15 minutes before you go to sleep, and again when you wake up will ultimately save time, energy, and increase your quality of life. I prefer to listen to guided visualization recordings or soothing music through head phones. I start with an intention to receive whatever I need at the time. After I am as comfortable as possible, with my eyes closed and rolled to the back of my head, I begin with a few deep cleansing breaths until I sink deeper into relaxation and stillness, silently repeating the chosen intention/mantra over and over if my mind starts to wander.

A strong practice of meditation can allow you powerful insight, and a mindful alignment with the wisdom of your soul. It is a perfect way to relax long enough to detach from the human details, and emerge with the most loving observer inside of you. Meditation should feel like a blissful freedom of knowing all is well, as you recharge in the comfort and clarity of the present moment. For those who want to, you can telepathically connect with the spiritual energy of your loved ones, no matter where they are.

There is no need to wait for a relaxing getaway, a spiritual healer, or a vortex of energy to bring you back into alignment. The beauty of meditation is that it can happen at any time you choose, where ever you are. When you are committed to mental, physical, and emotional wellbeing, it is an inside job above all else. Enlightenment is when you are living the powerful proof of all that you know now. This is when the party truly gets started.

It's extremely helpful to personalize the methods of grounding and centering that you resonate with most. Simply going through the motions of ritual and routine, as you work through your personal development checklist, is not the way that will truly offer long lasting benefit below the surface. The bottom line is, if something isn't fun, or doesn't feel good when you do it, you will not be likely to keep doing it for very long. You can push yourself to do it anyway, but it just feels like a chore, or just another thing to add to the "should" list.

This is true with every aspect in your life whether it's a job, a relationship, or health and fitness. You name it, in order to really have complete value and satisfaction, you must enjoy it. Instead of looking for the motivation to stay on task, begin by feeling your way to fun and inspiration and then take action.

Honestly, it really doesn't take that much prodding to see eyes light up when I tap into someone's core visions of bliss. The difficult part is moving people through internal resistance and into full belief of their own power. It is a life-changing realization when you discover that an exciting world of endless possibilities is only a few thoughts away.

Contrary to what most of us have been expected to believe about work, success, money, and security, the safest and surest course to your passion and purpose is to be authentically you. The "hard work" for all of us is really maintaining the thrilling connection with the truth of our soul. Constantly honoring the intuitive guidance we were born with is how you stay true to who you are. As we know, the Law of Attraction will match our energy with the perfect people and chain of events, validating the answers to our questions and solutions to our problems.

The only thing that can really ever hold us back from achieving anything we envision is our own fear: fear that it's too late; fear that we are handicapped, challenged, or damaged in some way; fear that we are not capable or not worthy; fear it would take financial abundance or extreme circumstances to be able to live our dreams; fear of being disappointed; fear of failure; fear of success; fear of outgrowing our current roles or relationships; fear of (fill in the blank). Regardless of the hurdle, entertaining doubt and lack of full belief in self is the truest block to everything we want.

I encourage everyone I consult with, to wait on committing to major decisions until they are in complete clarity of mind and positive emotional energy. Until then, choose the most accessible and appropriate way to enhance your current reality. You do not have to map out the rest of your life when you are 18, and you certainly don't have to stick to one plan. All you need to do is follow the most pleasing path available to you right now.

I think the golden ticket for most people is the freedom to enjoy the ultimate human experience, overflowing with love, family, friends, health, wealth, and a sense of purpose. This is actually a birthright given to all of us, not just those born with a silver spoon or the secret wisdom of the universe. Believing you have to wait to win the lottery in order to be generous, happy, and carefree will keep you trapped in a holding pattern for an entire lifetime.

Regardless of what you have believed and endured up to this point, your story is not over. Until you can completely identify with who you are, and the part you play in the big picture of humanity, you will typically follow the most logical and practical course. Inevitably, if you are not enjoying what you are doing for most of the hours in the day, you are ultimately cheating yourself out your own fortune of wellbeing. You are not here to conform to the path of another, you are here to exist as you evolve in the human experience.

When I talk about doing work that feeds your soul, it has nothing to do with the material world. Although the Law of Attraction always supports the soul's journey, there will never be enough money, houses, cars, clothes, or trips that will override the spirit's need to be free. Every single one of us has immediate access to unlimited abundance when we are operating from the love of our soul, not the fear of our ego.

Encourage children to stay true to the music that makes them sing and dance, instead of training them to march to the beat of one drummer. With the best of intentions, we can steer our loved ones in the direction of an illusionary safety net in hopes that they will always be securely protected. The wisest parents know that it is not our job to dictate the nature of our child's spirit, nor is it their job to please us. Our role is to be a guiding example, to ultimately show them how to fly confidently on their own.

There are far too many people in society who spend the majority of their time and energy doing work for the sake of other people. Yes, there is something to be said for the selfless efforts to make everyone around us happy and well taken care of. However, if we ourselves are not at the top of the list of our priorities, we are not truly offering, or receiving the full benefit of our being.

No matter what physical action you force yourself into, your strongest underlying belief about what you're doing is the signal to the universe for everything that comes back to you. If you think you cannot combine the joy of your passion with the flow of money, think again. The first thing you need to do is release all beliefs that tell you otherwise.

Referring back to the ultimate mindset, the more positive traits you allow to tip the scale, the more you tap into the vortex of love, wisdom, and abundance. The most incredible part, as you move closer and closer to the experience of "heaven on earth," you actually become less attached to the needs of the ego and earthly possession of things. You find yourself less concerned about accomplishing the goals and objectives, and more eagerly excited about having the time of your life in the process of getting there. This is true freedom.

If you are anything like me, and have spent your entire life attempting to squeeze into a reality of "normal" that has never fit you. It's time to stop. There are those of us who have always felt we are here for bigger reasons, but had no idea what those reasons were. We tended to think differently than almost anyone we knew and had a dominant voice inside of us constantly calling on us to make a difference in the world. We have taken many paths that seemed to lead nowhere, however, all of them have led us to our greater purpose. For you, the best is definitely yet to come and your time to walk in the truth of your shining light starts right now.

The individuals who often feel the most lost, tortured, and uncomfortable in their own skin, are actually the most brilliant, gifted, and talented humans on the planet. Some of us have faced enormous challenges and obstacles since the day we were born.

The most inspiring and motivational stories have been from those who overcame all odds to be an example of courage and love for humanity. It was necessary to know how to heal and love ourselves from the inside out to be the knowing guide leading the others from their darkness to their light.

The people and circumstances in our lives right now will tell us everything we need to know if we can only be open enough to see it and hear it. Let everyone and everything that crosses your path be the cues from a greater intelligence to get your attention. Do people come to you for your wisdom and advice? Do they ask you to fix household electronics or mechanical things? Do several people point out the same things about you again and again?

Is there something that seems natural to you that leaves others baffled or in awe of you? Are you most comfortable with numbers, people, animals, things, or nature? Where do you find yourself escaping to in your mind? What do you allow yourself to envision when money and time are no obstacles? What hobbies and favorite pastimes do you gravitate toward to have fun, relax, and recharge? You will find all of your answers and more when you look deep inside the perfect crystal ball which is you!

Life is not a game to see who can outsmart time as you race for the pot of gold, the fountain of youth, or the perfect partner. There is no one you have to compete with or compare yourself to. When you do you miss out on your good fortune along the way.

For the most part, we will fall into at least one, or even all, of the following categories: we will be taken care of by someone else's work; we will work for someone else; or we will work for ourselves. The avenue of income which will support our current priorities and lifestyle best is often the one we will stay the most loyal to. This can be exactly where the internal disconnect begins for those who are doing an incredible job at caring for their loved ones, and still not feeding their soul.

If you are one who has always seen yourself as the boss, then stick to that objective and create a plan that supports it. If you see yourself more as one who doesn't want to be in charge of anyone but yourself, then stay true to that dream and follow the path of least resistance in order to manifest your vision. You are the one who is really in charge of your future, so why not move in the direction of upmost enjoyment along the way.

As someone who was already trying to become financially independent by third grade, I have had a full range of experiences in the workplace as well as multiple attempts at self-employment. I grew up poor, but I wasn't really motivated by money, I was always driven by the thrill of the chase. Money was just a means to an end for me, even at that age.

I remember walking to elementary school one winter morning. I saw a blue object peeking out from some melted snow. It was a brand new case of mini Avon sample lipsticks. There must have been 50 different shades.

My first thought was to take it to school and sell each lipstick for a dime to my classmates as well as to my friends and the girls at recess. The word spread so fast that by lunchtime I had sold every one. The girls who missed out were so angry and disappointed, that the day ended with a return of everyone's money and a phone call to my parents to put on a lid on my entrepreneurial efforts.

Since my youth, I have started ten different businesses of my own, as well as continuously working full time for "the man." I have spent most of my days trying to figure out how to afford my own freedom. At the same time, deep down I understood it was something that money could never buy.

I always knew that creating a livelihood out of my truest passions was what I wanted. I just had no clue how to line it up into one path of success, not to mention maintaining it. When I decided to come out of the crazy closet, I knew I was opening myself up to be scrutinized by every belief system in the world. I just didn't care anymore. Worrying about what other people think of me was already destroying me. What did I really have to lose?

I was willing to walk through any remaining fear in order to be free. I put myself on public display and humbly disclosed the powerful intuition that I had tried to hide my whole life. Letting people know I could instantly see how they thought, and feel how they felt, was a claim I knew I could stand by. However, now I was ready to take everything to the next level.

I want to teach people not only how to love themselves more, but how to get excited about doing it. I just didn't know I would also be my own student in the process. That's when I started writing about everything I was discovering and literally wrote my way to freedom and full belief in myself. I became my own most challenging project as the most difficult part of all of my job was to allow people to pay me to do what I love, something so natural and gratifying that it never felt like work.

Regardless of the roles or duties we fulfill, even if we are paid for our efforts, we are all making an influential impact on ourselves, our families, our neighborhoods, and our communities. We are not really benefitting anyone, especially ourselves, by committing to a life of faking happiness, settling, or sacrificing ourselves. Choosing to stay dedicated to a healthy mind, body, and soul also means we become the living proof for all to witness. When we are completely living in our truth, loving who we are and what we do, we will truly experience amazing adventures in a beautiful kingdom.

In the big picture, we are all here better to serve nature, humanity, and all of creation. In one way or another, everything and everyone overlaps and affects every aspect of our planet and beyond. The simplest and most random acts of kindness have the strongest potential to influence the world for the better. Our universe is created, operated, and transformed through vibration. Even weather changes are impacted by mass consciousness of like-minded energy.

The best guidance you can ever receive, in order to live a life of passion and purpose, is to honor who you are and follow your bliss, incorporating more and more of an ultimate positive mindset and eliminating any self-defeating thoughts, words, and actions. Release the need to please and impress any other as you make decisions about the rest of your life. Prioritize your wellbeing to be just as important, if not more, as anything else. Allow full trust and belief in you to matter more than the validation of any others. Love yourself enough to allow your free spirit to fly.

Chapter 11: A New Naked: Authentic Intimacy

Deeper connections always seem to be at the top of most peoples' wish list. Honestly that's exactly why I positioned this chapter after all of the ways to fall in love with your own life first. The most solid and gratifying relationships will always be when you are already doing a great job at running your own life, self-aware and capable of managing your own mind and emotions extremely well.

I created this analogy to help keep our relationships in proper perspective:

> Life is basically our own amusement park created
> by the mind. We can ride whatever ride we want, as
> many times as we like, either alone or with friends.
> Some rides are thrilling and terrifying, all at the
> same time. Other rides offer a joyful pleasing to the
> soul, expanding our senses and imagination. It really
> just depends on what we choose to experience each
> day. We will interact with many people as they come
> and go along the way. We will enjoy playing with

some more than others, but they can all offer their own kind of fun. At the end of the day, we are left with our own thoughts and emotions. We can cry ourselves to sleep in the disappointing belief that our fun had to come to an end, or we can peacefully drift off into slumber with appreciation for another day of discovery.

When you are genuinely ready for the adventure of more meaningful and playful connections, you will not find them in the world of egos and insecurity. Where love is an intense ride of twists and turns, offering adrenaline-fueled highs, and death-defying lows. If you have found yourself trapped on the roller coaster of soaring into love, and then falling into loneliness, you now have more than enough empowering information and tools to begin a new reality of authentic intimacy.

First, let's revisit the universal truth about love, which can easily apply to everyone and every situation. Love is an invisible and all encompassing, vibrational energy, expressed and experienced in multiple ways to please the human senses and beyond. What we can see, touch, hear, smell and taste, is always so much better when compounded by the powerful surge of love. No matter how many ways humans will attempt to implement rules and conditions, love remains unlimited, and is eternally free flowing for all. Love is the source and the center of our universe.

Now you will be able to leverage the powerful truth of universal laws, in order to experience authentic intimacy by design. Keep in mind, this is a daily practice of applying and observing, and then applying and observing some more. The objective is progress, not perfection, deliberately creating the rest of your life and relationships from the easiest and most natural flow of wellbeing. Allow your new awareness, especially in regard to the Law of Attraction and an ultimate mindset, to be the starting point to anything you desire.

Regardless if you have been in a committed relationship with the same person for multiple years, started dating, are single or somewhere in between, you always have the choice to focus your intentions on appreciating your life exactly as it is in the present. Especially if you are considering any life altering decisions, the best place to start is in a mental state of clarity and emotional agreement. The most productive conversations you can have with your loved ones are when you allow the time to make peace with your own truth first.

You can commit to new promises, anytime "I do" turns to "I doubt," or the honeymoon light starts to fade. Always remember who you fell in love with, discerning whether you are still treating each other as best friends, and not worst enemies. Love is the answer to every question, as well as the starting point to resolve any problem. The secret ingredient to the recipe of compatible partnerships is to allow the best of you to show up, no matter the challenges you are faced with.

Authentic intimacy is the ongoing commitment to nurture more love and truth between you. Offering kindness over criticism, acceptance over annoyance, encouragement over confinement, fun over fighting, honesty over avoidance, and laughter over tears. We bond with others by being willing to be seen on the inside, not by repeatedly presenting the mask of a pretty package, or expecting to see one.

If you desire this depth of real and raw relating, it is imperative that you remain true to who you are and what really matters most to you. If you commit to join your life with another, you are hopefully already operating with a mindset which makes it easy to stay true to your promises, whether together or apart. Until you know that you are completely ready to stand by your agreements, without a shadow of a doubt, you are not yet in the position to make them.

Regardless if you choose to marry, live together, maintain separate finances or households, making it work means more than just saying "I love you." There also exists a higher road of responsibility to honor the energy of respect, appreciation, and tender loving care in all you say and do with your partner. The more ways you join your worlds together, the deeper the need for genuine transparency in anything that could impact the other.

This is a new kind of naked with the people we share our life with. An open window for another to view our personal journey from the inside out. Excitedly allowing further insight of each other's expanding perspective, agreeing to a new plan of action, when and if there is a disconnection between us. We must confidently and compassionately allow our loved one the beauty and strength found from managing their own emotions.

When you are mindfully managing your own life and direction, it is easier to know who is a bonus or a burden to your path. You will begin to instantly recognize when you are getting in your own way, or not living up to what you know now. As you release unhealthy patterns of relating, you will naturally be attracted to those with the same level of awareness or higher.

Hopefully by now, the one you appreciate most, is you. Without that, there isn't a solid foundation to build everlasting intimacy with any other. When you know how to be your own best friend, you automatically demonstrate how you prefer to be treated by anyone you encounter.

No matter if you have been in the same boat with someone for 50 years, or swimming in the sea of singles, embrace every moment to fall more in love with your own life. When you allow the necessary time to be with you, and recharge in positive energy, you are actually a much better friend, partner and lover. Learn to enjoy the space between you, as much as your time together. You will experience a new excitement making the absence into another opportunity for your heart to grow fonder.

The truest love, which every human is made of and has ability to access, is connection with the highest version and/or source of us. Unfortunately, most are convinced this can only be found in the arms of another. Granted, we often do not recognize the electric wave of "falling in love" quite like we do as the mutual attraction of an incredible mate. The difficulty arises if we expect the recipient of our affection, to make us always the object of their desire.

The secret to getting the most value and least amount of disappointment from any relationship is accepting that the direction to genuine connections is found from the inside out. It's knowing that love will always feel light, bright, natural, and free. It's trusting that each relationship has a bigger meaning and is an important part of our process regardless of duration.

In order to offer and receive the most benefit in your partnerships, there must be a commitment to growth and expansion of each individual. More importantly is the application and practice of that alignment in daily interactions. Fostering a mutual respect for each other's joy and journey will allow the freedom needed to expand even further, for the increased value of the relationship.

Regardless of who comes and goes in our lifetime, when we accept the universal guidance of love, we can never lose. We can breathe life, love, and laughter into all beginnings, as well as find peace, comfort, and strength at any ending. Just as you naturally formed through the umbilical cord attached to your mother, we are all connected to an invisible channel of life giving energy at all times. Knowing our own strength of character, and the higher truth through the eyes of love, we can never truly be hurt by another.

When we deliberately commit to live our lives on a higher road of intention, operating from an enlightened spirit, we will inevitably be attracted to equally evolving playmates: those who also honor exceptional care of their mind, body, and emotions; those whose lives, words and actions are beautifully aligned with the ultimate mindset they are committed to.

Most people make relationships far more complicated than necessary. To keep it simple, if you are currently in a committed and happy relationship, keep doing what you're doing. If you are single and having the time of your life, keep doing what you're doing. If you are still waiting and hoping for someone to save you from your loneliness, please keep practicing the art of self-appreciation and know how to rescue yourself first.

Here's what happens when two people are positively aligned in mind, body and soul. There is an instant and magnetic attraction. You will both have a natural easiness of compatibility and comfort as if you have known each other before and a mutual willingness to explore deeper levels of intimacy with another person. The Law of Attraction is better than any dating site out there.

There really is no better way to find genuine connections, other than modeling the positive elements of everything you admire, appreciate, and are impressed by in others. The most beneficial match will always be more like you than not. The special someone who "gets" how you think, encourages you to fly, and knows how to help you stay grounded will be the incredible mind mate who captures your attention and attraction on every level. The key is for each to stay committed to their own individual development, as well as the most beneficial path to walk with or without each other.

To prepare for this level of playing field, you must stay true to who you are. All relationships can then become a positive experience no matter what. Learn to trust yourself and it will be easier to know who to trust. Keep your focus on what you love, appreciate, and respect about everyone you know and continue to meet. Be the person you are looking for and the perfect soul will cross your path.

Mind games cannot exist if there is authentic intimacy. There will never be any need to place conditions or expectations on a return policy of love from anyone. You will want to treat everyone as valuable and deserving of love at all times, especially you. The more you let go of rules and requirements, the freer you are to enjoy and attract more positive experiences to you. The most attractive people on the planet are those who instantly recognize the internal beauty in each soul they meet.

This genuine transparency with another soul, expands the senses and frees your spirit, creating the safest platform to explore fun, friendship, and romantic intimacy with someone you adore. You will become two responsible and healthy adults, openly and honestly communicating and navigating through each new day with love.

How do I love thee? Let me count 7 ways, in 7 days, that you can attract authentic intimacy, or light the fire of a dying flame.

1. Look for opportunities to be thoughtful. When you spend time with your intended, listen carefully to the little things that make them happy. A future gesture that you listened and remembered, will mean more for your connection than the most expensive gifts. You will capture their heart every time you inspire their eyes to light up.

2. Be Kind. Use words that will empower the other. Sometimes out of fear, hurt, and anger, we will lash out at our partners in an effort to relieve our own discomfort. Always remember the people who love you are the ones who deserve your kindness the most.

3. Tell your partner something you like or love about them that's especially specific to their individual character. As the years roll by, we tend to take our loved ones for granted. Remind each other of the magic you fell in love with to begin with.

4. Spend time away from the day-to-day grind. Weekend getaways, new adventures, common interests, traveling to new sights are ideas to explore. Spend more time in fun and you will have less time for fighting.

5. Be your partner's best friend no matter what. When you are with your best friend you will be able to walk through anything together. Your best friend enjoys being with you more than anyone else. Your best friend understands you on a much deeper level. Your best friend encourages you to feel safe, comfortable, and free to be exactly who you are.

6. Make a deliberate intention to say what you mean, and mean what you say. When words and actions are in conflict with each other it only creates confusion and upset; whether communicated or not. Speak the truth with loving intention, and let the chips fall where they may. We do not help anyone when we attempt to protect them from their own feelings.

7. One of the best ways you can show love for your partner is to take care of yourself. When you neglect your health, your dreams, and your own life, you set yourself up for resentment and regret. The best partnerships are between those who know how to manage and prioritize the needs of their own mind, body, and soul. Know your boundaries and let no one be an exception to your golden rules.

Chapter 12: One for All and All for One

Okay, ladies and gentlemen, the time has come to walk your talk and apply what you know from the inside out. Your mission… when you choose to accept it, is first and foremost, to honor the well-being of your own mind, body, and spirit as your top priority. Then, and only then, is it possible to be the shining light who can fearlessly lead others out of their darkness. There are no words of wisdom that will ever have as much impact on you as the proof of your own life experiences.

In case you haven't noticed by now, I no longer believe anything is bad, wrong, a mistake, a coincidence, a fluke, or an accident. Nor do I still find the need to seek explanations in labels, conditions, disabilities, handicaps, syndromes, diagnoses, or disease. To the contrary, I believe we all choose the perfect start, as well as all of our so called character defects and personal challenges in this lifetime. I also know we have the natural and powerful ability to create a reality of perfect health, because I have done it.

In fact, the assumed obstacles that can initially pull us down like quicksand, actually are the basis for our greater purpose in this time and space. There really is no need to feel sorry for other people, as I'm certain every soul knows exactly what their spiritual goal is in this lifetime. It's just a matter if we choose to be the human example of self-will run riot, or the human example of unconditional love for one and all. The majority fall somewhere in between.

I'm assuming if you made it to these words, you are more than ready to be free of the old world mentality and ancient ways of doing things. Since the universe is already set up so perfectly, we are given the natural separation of rest and wakefulness. Day to night, light to dark, always bringing a new day and fresh start to begin again with what we know now.

This means you get to have a lifelong journey of being mindfully present and more awake every time you open your eyes. You stop wasting time rehashing a past, that can only be changed in your own mind anyway, or fearfully looking into a future that is actually being formed through your present beliefs. You have complete awareness that you are the only one creating your own reality. Now you will be able to leverage this information to prove it to yourself.

The best path is the one which allows you to be who you are naturally. Following your bliss, rather than conforming to the requirements, expectations, and opinions of anyone else. The most beneficial strategy for a healthy and prosperous life is to start with an ultimate positive mindset. At the same time, trusting the insightful guidance of your intuition to move forward.

This is guiding communication from the voice of your soul, always knowing the highest and best direction for you.

No matter the subject, the vibrational direction of your thoughts, is the beginning and the end to everything and the validation if you have been focused on negative, fear-based beliefs if you are currently experiencing upheaval or disharmony in any area of your life. The proof that you have been giving attention to positive, love-based thinking, is when you notice everything is lining up in your favor very quickly. Therefore, anytime you find yourself in mental confusion and negative emotion, take time out, and realign your thinking to a place of greater emotional relief.

When you are on purpose, there is an incredible sense of well-being and satisfaction within. A humble confidence as you move into full belief of yourself, enjoying and appreciating the life that you are creating. Becoming more willing to stop and smell the beautiful roses, and less likely to see the thorns.

Many are waking up all around us. They are the ones who are exuberantly shouting this message to anyone who will listen. The secret to life, the key to love, the path to abundance are all available to everyone right now! You want to believe it's as possible for you, but if your current reality says otherwise, you also want to scream F.U. in the face of Mr. or Mrs. Sunshine.

As someone who finally turned my frown upside down, I can testify that the truth only hurts when you are not ready to see it. The next time you feel negative emotion as a result of another person's words or actions, do your best to acknowledge the emotion and then set it aside in order to take a deeper look inside. These are the perfect opportunities to be forever free of the chains that bind you. To truly be free in your awakening, you will need to shed your final layer of protection. In other words, the invisible wall you built thicker and taller after years of disappointment and devastation. All of those times you told yourself not to get too excited, hopeful, or emotionally available because of all the times you felt heartbroken, devastated, humiliated, foolishly vulnerable, used, and taken for granted. When you ask for more, and are truly ready to take life to the next level, you will be shown exactly what part of you is standing in your way.

Trust me, I have been chiseling away at my own fortress for quite some time. I assure you, the fastest way to absolute freedom is to begin by letting go of everything that makes you feel bad about yourself when you think it, say it, or do it; the mean and critical things we tell ourselves as we portray our worst enemy. The self-defeating behaviors that match the negative thoughts we are thinking of ourselves and others. The words we choose to reflect, or deflect, our deeper truth. The disrespectful and hurtful ways we allow others to treat us. I've done it all, and I see pieces of all of it in others.

Everyone who shows up in our life, including loved ones who were born before us, are all extensions of us, as we are extensions of them. We are not here to change the world or to get everyone to think the same way. We are actually here to work with the information that can only be recognized through the many differences between us. If everyone were exactly alike, and every day the same, how could we ever expand and evolve? What would be the purpose for life and discovering new ways to coexist?

What every spiritually evolved being comes to know, is that we are all from the same energy source. We are all created from a higher frequency of love, divided into physical variations to experience relativity. When we hate another we hate ourselves. This is the whole eye for an eye philosophy, unfortunately the principle gets distorted as a reason for revenge. What it really means is that law of attraction will always match like energy, with like energy. You will get back everything you give out by natural law, commonly referred to as Karma.

I have talked to enough people by now to make the following bold statements. Humans are actually more alike than we are different. We are drawn to the people who have the traits we want to see in ourselves. We make our relationships into hard work because we pretend like we don't know how impossible it is for our partner to stay perfect for us. Initially, it's easier to assign blame to others for our so called problems, because it feels a little better than blaming ourselves. At the end of the day we will always know the real truth.

Well, now's your chance to be different. You get to give everyone a get out of jail free card, including you, for life. All you really need to do is keep your side of the street clean and leave everyone else to their own business. Even minor children only need so much care and supervision, then it's best to give them the age-appropriate space to safely explore their world from behind their own eyes. You will be pleasantly surprised with the amount of time and energy you have left over when you stop catering to everyone else's needs, and start taking more care of you.

You can search places, people, and things for the answers to your questions, but your solutions will always be found when you look in the universal mirror of truth. If you have spent any amount of time on earth, you already know what it will take to create the life you dream of, as well as what it will take to end any misery. It's a matter of aligning with the mindset that will ultimately work best to get you there, and then applying the practice of these traits in every conscious minute of your days.

I like to keep things simple because they really are. Your past does not determine one bit of your future, but it is the perfect experience to show you who you are today, and what you prefer now. You are the clock and the calendar, always the determining factor as to how long something, or someone, will take to appear in your physical reality.

The delays and detours will be any time you dive back into fear and negative beliefs. What you strive to achieve is much sweeter when you appreciate the difficulties you were able to overcome in order to get there. You will never get it all done, and you never intended to… Life goes on, and so do you.

The universal mind is at our beck and call so we need to be very clear and in positive belief when we ask for anything, staying in appreciation and excitement during the process, and calmly detached from the need to control the timing and outcome. Stretching yourself to be the highest version of you will always pay off.

The relationships and experiences we have along the way are not by coincidence and yet, are not a preset fate or destiny. They are, however, exactly what's needed to validate if we are on our truest path. It is the wise and the few who will actually listen to the information as it shows up in their own lives, and leverage the awareness for the betterment of all. The soul doesn't care about details or duration, the soul is always ready to love.

Many will nod in agreement but very few will fully embrace the power of their own mind. When you do, you also become a part of the smallest percentage of the population who live in full belief of all that is possible. The knowing that you have the ability to manifest instantly and the power to create worlds. The happiest, healthiest, and wealthiest are those who are awake, aware and tapped into complete abundance for one and all.

I want to share one final personal experience about the power of belief. It was May 2015, I had almost two years under my belt of working 50-plus hours a week in a role I had hated for 20 years, and I was trying to create an entirely new life at the same time. Weekends and holidays were spent building a name for myself as an Intuitive Consultant and writing this book in any spare time I had left over. I was also riding the emotional roller coaster of dealing with my son's addiction in full blown status, as well as grieving the loss of two pets and several people I have loved for most of my life. Needless to say, I was burning the candle at both ends.

One busy Saturday afternoon in Jerome, I decided to take a much needed break from back to back readings. It had just started to rain and I hesitated to take my normal route to fresh air. I ignored the inner voice and decided to venture down the private emergency stairs off the back of the building. I will spare you the gory details but after just a few steps, the heel of my boot slipped perfectly in a hole on the grated step. I reached for the handrail but lost my grip as the rest of my body went down. Hanging by one foot, with 12 feet of steel grated steps and cement below, I wiggled my foot free and rolled down the stairs until I smashed my head into the grated fence below.

The results were staples in my head, massive bleeding and bruising with a damaged left ankle, but I was alive. As I recovered that summer, I knew I had experienced my last wakeup call. I could no longer keep pushing myself beyond the limits without knowing there would be dire consequences. Not in my work, not in my relationships, and not with my own mind and body. It was time to recover, from the inside out.

For three months, I hobbled from one doctor to the next in hopes someone might be able to fix my ankle. I was still using crutches, and experiencing swelling and pain every night. I was determined to have my active lifestyle back, and even more important, to dance at my oldest son's upcoming wedding. I decided I would test the power of belief and the Law of Attraction to manifest a healer who could help me. A few weeks later, that's exactly what happened.

Again, it was a busy Saturday in Jerome. I was in the middle of a conversation when a man walked in and abruptly asked to have a reading. I felt strangely intrigued as I did a quick personal safety check and agreed to see him. Shortly into my consultation, I knew he was silently reading me and when I asked him about it, he started smiling and nodded. I then asked what he was really doing here and he said he was sent by a psychic he went to in Phoenix. She told him to go to Jerome and he would find more validation for his calling.

Suddenly I could see his Native American features as he explained his need to confirm what his tribal elders were always convinced of. They knew he was a natural born spiritual healer or shaman. Many label these individuals as a "medicine man or medicine woman," referring to the belief that we can heal without medicine. Oddly, just like me, he had not stepped into full belief of his gift and thought I might have answers for him.

At this point, he had not seen that was I injured and I always made every effort to not bring any attention to it. Nor did he appear to be anything more than an average, middle-aged Joe off the street. Once he started opening up to me, I told him about my fall and that I was still struggling.

He asked me to put my foot on his knee and I did. He said he was going to circle his hand above the injury and I would receive a vision of the true source of the pain. I closed my eyes and, although he never touched my foot, I began to feel the sensation of heat on the affected area. In a matter of seconds I saw a series of pictures flashing through my mind like snapshots of memories all at the same time. In unison, I said "I see it!" and he said, "I got it!"

It was only a matter of 15 minutes, but felt like a life time of release. I began sobbing uncontrollably and he waited patiently and compassionately. When I could regain my composure, he gave me a hug, thanked me for seeing him and left as fast as he came. That night, for the first time in over three months, my foot didn't swell up. Three days later, I was walking without a limp.

I still think about that day all the time. I was left with a mark on that spot that resembles the letter M. Every time I look at it I am reminded of the magic and mastery that is possible when I have full belief. I never got the gentleman's name and I have not seen him since. I didn't get to tell him what he did for me and that he truly is a healer, yet somehow I have a feeling he already knows. In all honesty, I'm not even sure he was from this dimension. What I do know, is the truth would finally set me free. The overwhelming upheaval of anything and everything that was holding me back from true connection with my own soul. I was literally keeping one foot stuck in the old world of pain and suffering. Just like my friend, I was still not convinced of my own powerful gift, or living in complete belief of me, until that day.

What did I see? I saw the raw and real truth in every relationship, life circumstance, and destructive belief I had ever had. I also knew everything I would need to let go of in order to move forward. It was at this time that I dedicated the rest of my life to teaching unconditional love, and it was going to start with me. For the next several months, I put everything and everyone on hold that I possibly could. I dealt with only the details of my life that were the most pressing and necessary. The rest of my focus was solely on healing any past fears and old wounds, that were still surfacing. Determined to become the healer of my own pain and the strongest guide to my own empowerment. I learned how to fall in love with life and appreciate who I have become through it all.

I realize there are still skeptics in the world, as I happened to be the biggest one of all, for a very long time. Until you have a deep knowing and the undeniable proof of your own experiences, it is difficult to take the words of anyone else; even people you love and trust. That is why I do not waste time trying to convince people to believe me. To the contrary, my mission is for all souls to believe in themselves.

The mechanics of how life works, are really very basic and simple. We are all creating our lives with our own minds. We all have a different view from behind our own eyes. We are all love, at the very core of us, and connected to the same energy as the source of all creation. Do you want to see more love and peace in the world? Be the example, choose to see only love, speak words of love, think thoughts of love, and behave in loving ways. Welcome to Awakening! The possibilities of happy endings are infinite.